HODGES LIBRARY

P9-DZA-246

Basic

American

Grammar

and Usage

An ESL/EFL Handbook

Marcel Danesi, Ph.D.

University of Toronto

BARRON'S

Copyright © 2006 by Barron's Educational Series, Inc.

All rights reserved. No part of this book may be reproduced in
any form, by photostat, microfilm, xerography, or any other
means, or incorporated into any information retrieval system,
electronic or mechanical, without the written
permission of the copyright owner.

All inquiries should be addressed to:
Barron's Educational Series, Inc.
250 Wireless Boulevard
Hauppauge, New York 11788
www.barronseduc.com

ISBN-13: 978-0-7641-3358-9
ISBN-10: 0-7641-3358-6

Library of Congress Catalog Card No.: 2005048088

Library of Congress Cataloging-in-Publication Data
Danesi, Marcel, 1946–
    Basic American Grammar and Usage: An ESL/EFL Handbook /
by Marcel Danesi.— 1st ed.
    ISBN-13: 978-0-7641-3358-9
    ISBN-10: 0-7641-3358-6
    1. English language—Textbooks for foreign speakers. 2. English
language—Grammar—Handbooks, manuals, etc. I. Title: ESL/EFL
handbook. II. Title.

PE1128.D296   2006
428.2′4—dc22   2005048088

Printed in the United States of America

9 8 7 6 5 4 3 2 1

Contents

Preface

In a letter dated September 5, 1918, the great Irish writer James Joyce (1882–1941) wrote the following words: "Writing in English is the most ingenious torture ever devised for sins committed in previous lives." For many students of English As a Second Language (ESL) or English As a Foreign Language (EFL), Joyce's statement seems to ring particularly true!

The English language may be torture for writers, but it should not be so for students. This handbook is intended to take the torture away, in a manner of speaking, by providing a reference manual on the basic grammatical features of American English. As an ESL/EFL teacher myself, I have come to realize that it is important to flesh out those features that cause the greatest degree of difficulty to a large number of students and identify them precisely. This book is the result of many years of preparing materials designed to do exactly that. It is intended primarily to appeal to academically oriented young learners, although older learners might also find information in it that they too can use. Above all else, it is intended for "grammar phobics" of any age, defined as students who are put off by grammatical explanations that take too much background knowledge for granted.

Needless to say, there are many good reference books for ESL/EFL students on the market. But they are rarely written with the grammar phobic in mind, "conversing" with him or her in a straightforward way on the intricacies of grammar. This book is written in just such a "conversational style." It also contains exercises for immediate practice and control of each grammar topic. Keep in mind, however, that this is not a course book with a large variety of exercises such as those that are used in intensive study texts and courses. The exercises here are brief and to the point, designed to help you work in an uncomplicated manner with the concepts introduced in a particular section. This is primarily a handbook with a practical side to it. Nevertheless, when you add up the number of exercises in this text, you will find that there are as many as you will find in the more formal textbooks! Because they can be used as a tool for self-study, the exercises are written to produce precise answers (multiple choice, correct the errors, fill in the blanks, and so on). In this way, you can check your answers right away in the *Answers* section.

Basic American English Grammar and Usage is thus a blend of reference and self-study. If terms such as *participles*, *conjunctions*, and the like, "turn you off," as the expression goes, this book is for you. Nothing is taken for granted. Every technical term is explained and illustrated fully. And to make a grammatical topic more understandable, it is treated in "point form." By the way, there is no way around grammar if you are a serious ESL/EFL student! To become adept in a language you must know how its component parts work together. Imagine a chemist who cannot name chemicals by their technical names. You would hardly consider such a person a "proficient chemist." Grammatical terms, like technical terms in chemistry, put you in a better position to think about the English language in a logical and precise way. In other words, they allow you to become truly proficient in the language.

This book is one of a series of ESL/EFL handbooks published by Barron's Educational Series. A handbook is an important tool in the process of learning another language because it gives you the opportunity to reflect upon what you know, to reinforce your skills, to fill in gaps, to clarify difficult points—in sum, to build a firm knowledge of the language. But a handbook cannot do it all for you. This book is not an encyclopedic volume of all there is to know about the English language. Like the other handbooks in the series, it will give you only the basic facts, thus keeping the learning of the language within manageable proportions.

There are fifteen chapters in this handbook, covering everything from simple sentences to writing e-mails. Each chapter is designed to cover a main topic of grammar as completely as possible. Therefore, some chapters are longer than others. This is because of the varying number of features that a specific grammatical topic entails. For example, the chapter on verbs is longer than the one on adjectives and adverbs. Nevertheless, you will never find a chapter to be of an unwieldy length.

You can also read this book as if it were a "story"—the "grammatical story" of the English language. If you do, then you should start reading it from page one and work your way through it a little at a time. The book is designed to be sequential for that very reason. There are also cross-references to guide you along the way in the event you may have forgotten something. By the end of the story you will have an overall picture of how the grammatical bits and pieces fit together.

You can, of course, also use this book as a reference manual, using the table of contents and the index to guide you to the areas of grammar on which you need information. As helpful devices, sidebars are added throughout the book to clarify, supplement, or complement certain topics.

Marcel Danesi
University of Toronto, 2005

— 1 —

Sentences

The words of the world want to make sentences.

Gaston Bachelard (1884–1962)

What Is a Sentence?

1. A *sentence* is an organized series of words that allows you to make a statement, ask a question, express a thought, offer an opinion, and so on. In writing, a sentence starts with a capitalized word and ends with a period, a question mark, or an exclamation mark.

   That woman is American.
   Is that woman American?
   I am absolutely positive that she is American!

2. A sentence is organized in relation to what you intend to say and how you are going to say it. You cannot put words in just any order!

   Jumbled

   Woman that is American.
   American woman that is?

   Organized

   That woman is American.
   Is that woman American?

3. Sentences have two basic parts: a subject and a predicate. The *subject* is the part of sentence that denotes the doer of an action or what the sentence is about. It is often the first element in a simple sentence such as a direct statement. The *predicate* is the part of a sentence that provides information about the subject. In simple sentences, it comes after the subject:

   Subject

   That woman
   Carmen
   Your car

   Predicate

   is American.
   is studying French.
   consumes too much gas.

1

> ### Subject–Verb Agreement
>
> Sentence organization means in part that there is *agreement* between the subject and the verb of a sentence. If the subject is singular, the verb must also be singular; if it is plural, the verb must be plural:
>
> *Alex speaks English well.*
> *They speak English well.*
>
> Subjects made up of several nouns or noun phrases connected by *and* require a plural verb:
> *My brother and sister speak well.*
> *John and his friend are funny.*
>
> When *every* or *each* is used in the subject, the verb must be singular:
>
> *Every man, woman, and child speaks English well in this city.*
> *Each boy and girl in that school loves to study.*
>
> Note the agreement pattern when a phrase or clause is added to the subject:
>
> *My dog, as well as my cats, loves to eat cookies.*
>
> A "gerund subject" always requires a singular verb:
>
> *Raising children is a difficult task.*
>
> Subjects that are singular in meaning (even though they end in -s) require a singular verb:
> *The United States is a big place.*
> *Sears is a great store.*
>
> Subjects that are plural in meaning (even if they do not end in -s) require a plural verb:
>
> *People are funny.*
> *Cattle are domestic animals.*
>
> Adjectives used as subjects require a plural verb because they refer to a group of people:
>
> *The rich are all around us.*
> *The young are always so brash.*

4. But be careful! The subject is not always the first element in a sentence:

   Yes, <u>Marisa</u> is studying French.
   Does <u>your car</u> really consume a lot of gas?

5. A sentence can have more than one subject and / or predicate:

   Debbie thinks that you are Italian.
   That woman is the American lady who lives near us.

6. Each combination of subject and predicate is called a *clause*. In sentences consisting of more than one clause, there is a main clause, called an *independent clause*, and one or more subordinate clauses, called *dependent clauses*. The latter are usually introduced by words such as *that*, *which*, and so on.

   <u>*Debbie thinks*</u>   *that*   <u>*you are Italian*</u>.
       ↑   ↑
   Independent   Dependent
   clause   clause

7. A *compound sentence* is a sentence made up of two or more sentences, not clauses, linked together by words such as *and* and *or* called *conjunctions*:

   <u>*I speak English*</u> and <u>*my friend speaks Spanish*</u>.

8. A subject must contain a noun, a substantive (a word taking on the function of a noun), a noun phrase (a group of words consisting of a noun modified or specified by an article, demonstrative, adjective, and so on), or a pronoun; a predicate must include a verb. The "parts of speech" that make up the subject and predicate (nouns, verbs, and so on) are defined and discussed in subsequent chapters.

9. When speaking or writing, you do not always need to use complete sentences. Parts of a sentence may be left out when they are clearly implied:

   How are you?
   I am well, thanks.   or   *Well, thanks.*

   When did your father arrive?
   My father arrived at three o'clock.   or   *At three o'clock.*

   When did you go to the theater?
   I went to the theater yesterday.   or   *Yesterday.*

10. Sentences can also be constructed to emphasize something. In writing, emphatic sentences have an exclamation mark at the end. One method of constructing such a sentence is to use the verb *do* in its appropriate form and change the main verb to the infinitive. Another method is to change the word order around, bringing the emphatic part to the front of the sentence:

Nonemphatic	Emphatic
Louise <u>paid</u> the bill.	*Yes, Louise <u>did pay</u> the bill!*
He <u>came</u> to the movies, as well.	*Yes, he too <u>did come</u> to the movies!*
They left <u>quietly</u>, like thieves.	*<u>Quietly</u>, they left, like thieves!*

11. The imperative tense usually implies emphasis:

    Ann, pay the bill!
    Children, be quiet!
    Alex, eat all your vegetables!
    Sarah, drink all the milk!

12. Sentences can also be *active* or *passive*. In an active sentence, the subject of the sentence is performing the action expressed by the verb; in a passive sentence, the grammatical subject has the action of the verb performed on it. Passive forms will be discussed in Chapter 9:

Active

Mary <u>reads</u> the book.
Bill <u>will</u> <u>eat</u> the meat.

Passive

The book <u>is</u> <u>read</u> by Mary.
The meat <u>will</u> <u>be</u> <u>eaten</u> by Bill.

13. Some sentences are constructed to state quotations directly with quotation marks; others are constructed to report them indirectly with a subordinate clause:

Quoted speech

Carlo asks, "Are you Italian?"
Mary said, "I am coming too."

Reported speech

Carlo asked if you were Italian.
Mary said that she was coming too.

Exercise Set 1-1

A. Missing from the following sentences is either the appropriate punctuation or an agreement between the verb and the subject. Correct each sentence.

1. My friend is Italian!
2. Who is she.
3. Go away.
4. My friend and I speaks Spanish.
5. Each person in my house drive an American car.
6. The elderly is not necessarily wise.
7. The people in this city is always friendly.
8. Speaking many languages are difficult.
9. The United States are a great country.
10. Our dog, as well as our cat, are very friendly.
11. Yes, do it right away.
12. She asked me, Are you Spanish?
13. She asked me if "I were Spanish."
14. That pastry ate by Mary.

B. Identify each italicized part as being a subject, a predicate, an independent clause, or a dependent clause.

1. *Alex is majoring in mathematics.*
2. Sarah *is a great pianist.*
3. My parents think that *I am too young to get married.*
4. Our teacher is a person *who rarely gets angry.*
5. *Many people believe* that pollution is endangering everybody's health.

C. Choose the appropriate answer, (a) or (b):

1. How is it going?
   (a) I am going.
   (b) Very well, thanks.

2. Who called a minute ago?
   (a) Maria.
   (b) A minute ago.

3. At what time should we meet?
   (a) At two-thirty.
   (b) Let's meet.

4. Why did you say that?
   (a) Because I felt like it.
   (b) I said it.

Affirmative Sentences

1. An *affirmative sentence* (also known as a *statement* or a *declarative sentence*) is a sentence that allows you to state or affirm something in a straightforward way. In written speech, it has a period at the end:

He speaks English very well.
That girl plays the piano exceptionally well.
All our relatives live in Mexico.

2. The predicate of an affirmative sentence may or may not have an object. An *object* is the noun, substantive, noun phrase, or pronoun in a predicate that receives the action expressed by the verb:

   Mark calls every night (no object).

   Mark calls his fiancée every night.
   ↑
   object

   Mark has never written to her.
   ↑
   object

3. There are two types of objects: direct and indirect. You can identify each one very easily as follows:

   A *direct object* is a noun, substantive, noun phrase, or pronoun indicating what or who(m) the receiver of the action is:

   Mark calls his fiancée every night.
   ↑
   direct object
   (*Mark calls whom?*)

   An *indirect object* is a noun, substantive, noun phrase, or pronoun indicating to whom or for whom an action is intended:

   Mark has never written to her.
   ↑
   indirect object
   (*Mark has never written to whom?*)

4. Some verbs can be followed by both kinds of objects:

   Mark will dedicate a song to his fiancée.
   ↑   ↑
   direct   indirect
   object   object

5. If the indirect object precedes the direct object, the preposition is dropped (normally):

   Mark gave that CD to me.   or   *Mark gave me that CD.*
   Mark gave a CD to her yesterday.   or   *Mark gave her a CD yesterday.*

6. Verbs that normally require a direct object are called *transitive*:

> *Jorge also asked the professor to come.*
> *Gina is always phoning her mother.*
> *He always answers questions in class.*

7. Verbs that cannot be followed by a direct object are called *intransitive*:

> *My mother listens to the radio every evening.*
> *Mary is waiting for the bus.*
> *Tina is looking for her purse.*

> ### Transitive and Intransitive Verbs
>
> *Raise, set, ask, phone, answer,* and *lay* are transitive verbs:
>
> > *He raised his hand in class.*
> > *We set the book on the table.*
> > *Who set the table for lunch?*
>
> *Rise, listen, wait, look, sit,* and *lie* are intransitive verbs:
>
> > *The sun rises in the east.*
> > *We always sit near each other.*
> > *She is lying on the couch.*

8. Predicates can also consist of *complements*. These are words or phrases that follow a linking verb (*be, seem,* and so on) or answer questions such as those beginning with *Where* and *How*:

> *Mark went to work. (Where did Mark go?)*
> *Jane sat on the couch. (Where did Jane sit?)*
> *He is wonderful. (How is he?)*

9. Be careful! An object is not always needed:

> *The child is sleeping.*
> *They always call.*

10. In English (unlike in Spanish, Italian, and other languages), the subject slot must always be filled, even when no specific subject is involved. The "fillers" of subject slots, *it* and *there,* are known as *expletives.* They are sometimes called "dummy subjects." Note that *it* requires a verb in the singular. With *there* the verb can be singular or plural, depending on whether the ensuing noun phrase is singular or plural:

> *It is hot today.*
> *There is little time to do this.*
> *There are many CDs in my collection.*

Exercise Set 1-2

A.   Identify the verb as transitive (T), intransitive (I), or linking (L).

_____ 1. Maria waited for you all day yesterday.
_____ 2. She seems very happy.
_____ 3. I always ask my friend to go out with me on weekends.
_____ 4. Have you ever listened to the music of Mozart?
_____ 5. Give me your address, please!
_____ 6. Put it on the table!

B.   There is an error or a missing element in each sentence. Correct each one in an appropriate fashion.

1.   There is lots of people in this room.
2.   Are many cars on the road today. ?
3.   Debbie always sits the sofa to watch TV.
4.   I always wait him after school.
5.   She phones to me every day.
6.   He gave to her a gift for her birthday.
7.   We listened the radio together.
8.   Is correct, isn't it?

Negative Sentences

1.   A *negative sentence* allows you to deny, contradict, or refuse something:

Affirmative   **Negative**

He speaks English very well.   *He does not speak English very well.*
That girl plays the piano well.   *That girl does not play the piano well.*

2.   There are several ways to make sentences (and clauses) negative. If the sentence (or clause) is constructed with the verb *be*, put *not* after the verb. Verbs are discussed in Chapter 8:

Affirmative   **Negative**

That doctor is my cousin.   *That doctor is not my cousin.*
The children are sleepy.   *The children are not sleepy.*

3. Similarly, if the sentence or clause is constructed with a modal verb (*may go, will come,* and so on), a verb in a progressive tense (*is waiting, was sleeping*), or a verb in a perfect tense, including *be (has been)*, put the word *not* between the two main parts of the verb:

Affirmative	Negative

Modal:

Mary <u>may</u> <u>go</u> to France.	Mary <u>may</u> <u>not</u> <u>go</u> to France.
The child <u>should</u> <u>sleep</u> more.	The child <u>should</u> <u>not</u> <u>sleep</u> more.
They <u>will</u> <u>leave</u> tomorrow.	They <u>will</u> <u>not</u> <u>leave</u> tomorrow.

Progressive:

Mary <u>is</u> <u>waiting</u> for the bus.	Mary <u>is</u> <u>not</u> <u>waiting</u> for the bus.
The child <u>was</u> <u>sleeping</u> this morning.	The child <u>was</u> <u>not</u> <u>sleeping</u> this morning.
They <u>are</u> <u>leaving</u> tomorrow.	They <u>are</u> <u>not</u> <u>leaving</u> tomorrow.

Perfect:

Mary <u>has</u> <u>gone</u> to France.	Mary <u>has</u> <u>not</u> <u>gone</u> to France.
The child <u>had</u> <u>slept</u> a lot.	The child <u>had</u> <u>not</u> <u>slept</u> a lot.
I <u>have</u> <u>been</u> to France.	I <u>have</u> <u>not</u> <u>been</u> to France.

4. Use *do* + *not* + infinitive of the verb in all other cases. Notice that the tense of the affirmative verb is "taken on" by *do* and that the affirmative verb itself is changed to its infinitive form:

Affirmative	Negative
The doctor <u>said</u> it.	The doctor <u>did</u> <u>not</u> <u>say</u> it.
The child <u>sleeps</u> a lot.	The child <u>does</u> <u>not</u> <u>sleep</u> a lot.

5. Be careful! Unlike some languages, English does not allow a "double negative."

Correct	Incorrect
Don't touch anything!	*Don't touch nothing!*

Exercise Set 1-3

A. In the following sentences the word *not* is out of place. Put it in its correct slot.

1. He did do it not.
2. Our friends not have seen that movie.
3. She will be coming with us not.
4. You should eat so not many sweets.
5. They not are coming to the movies.
6. He not is American.
7. I not do understand what you are talking about.

B. Make each sentence negative.

1. My brother works at the library.
2. She can work at the library.
3. He goes to Princeton.
4. I believe you.
5. My sister also believed you.
6. I may do it.
7. I did it.

Interrogative Sentences

1. An *interrogative sentence* is one that allows you to ask questions, make inquiries, express doubts, and so on. In writing, it always has a question mark at the end, rather than a period. One way to form an interrogative sentence—although used infrequently—is simply to put a question mark at the end of a sentence with the structure of an affirmative sentence:

Affirmative	**Interrogative**
Ann is looking for the cat.	*Ann is looking for the cat?*
The child sleeps peacefully.	*The child sleeps peacefully?*
He always reads at night.	*He always reads at night?*

2. There are three main types of interrogative sentences. The first is known as a *yes / no question* because it is designed to elicit a *yes / no* answer (explicitly or implicitly). There are several ways to form *yes / no* questions. If the sentence is constructed with the verb *be*, the verb *be* itself is put at the beginning of the sentence. In a negative sentence, the word *not* can also be put after *be* and contracted with it (at the beginning):

Interrogative	**Response**
<u>Is</u> Ann your friend?	Yes, Ann <u>is</u> my friend.
	No, Ann <u>is</u> <u>not</u> my friend.
<u>Are</u> those children your cousins?	Yes, those children <u>are</u> my cousins.
	No, those children <u>are</u> <u>not</u> my cousins.

Negative interrogative	**Response**
<u>Isn't</u> Ann your friend?	Yes, Ann <u>is</u> my friend.
	No, Ann <u>is</u> <u>not</u> my friend.
<u>Is</u> Ann <u>not</u> your friend?	Yes, Ann <u>is</u> my friend.
	No, Ann <u>is</u> <u>not</u> my friend.
<u>Aren't</u> those children your cousins?	Yes, those children <u>are</u> my cousins.
	No, those children <u>are</u> <u>not</u> my cousins.
<u>Are</u> those children <u>not</u> your cousins?	Yes, those children <u>are</u> my cousins.
	No, those children <u>are</u> <u>not</u> my cousins.

3. If the sentence is constructed with a modal verb, a verb in a progressive tense, or a verb in a perfect tense, the first part of the verbal construction is put at the beginning. In a negative sentence, the word *not* can also be put after the relevant part and contracted with it (at the beginning):

Interrogative	**Response**
<u>Is</u> Ann <u>looking</u> for the cat?	Yes, Ann <u>is</u> <u>looking</u> for the cat.
	No, Ann <u>is</u> <u>not</u> <u>looking</u> for the cat.
<u>Was</u> the child <u>sleeping</u>?	Yes, the child <u>was</u> <u>sleeping</u>.
	No, the child <u>was</u> <u>not</u> <u>sleeping</u>.

Has his father *arrived* already?	Yes, his father *has arrived* already.
	No, his father *has not arrived* yet.
Should they *come* too?	Yes, they *should come* too.
	No, they *should not come*.
Can I *play* at your wedding?	Yes, you *can play* at our wedding.
	No, you *cannot play* at our wedding.

Negative Interrogative	**Response**
Isn't Ann *looking* for the cat?	Yes, Ann *is looking* for the cat.
	No, Ann *is not looking* for the cat.
Is Ann *not looking* for the cat?	Yes, Ann *is looking* for the cat.
	No, Ann *is not looking* for the cat.
Wasn't the child *sleeping*?	Yes, the child *was sleeping*.
	No, the child *was not sleeping*.
Was the child *not sleeping*?	Yes, the child *was* sleeping.
	No, the child *was not sleeping*.
Can't I *play* at your wedding?	Yes, you *can play* at our wedding.
	No, you *cannot play* at our wedding.
Can I *not play* at your wedding?	Yes, you *can play* at our wedding.
	No, you *cannot play* at our wedding.

4. In all other cases, *do + not + infinitive of the verb* is used at the beginning of the sentence. Notice that the tense of the main verb is "taken on" by *do* and that the verb itself is changed to its infinitive form:

Interrogative	**Response**
Does the child *sleep* peacefully?	Yes, the child *sleeps* peacefully.
	No, the child *does not sleep* peacefully.
Did he always *read* at night?	Yes, he always *read* at night.
	No, he never *read* at night.

Negative interrogative	**Response**
Doesn't the child *sleep* peacefully?	Yes, the child *sleeps* peacefully.
	No, the child *does not sleep* peacefully.
Does the child *not sleep* peacefully?	Yes, the child *sleeps* peacefully.
	No, the child *does not sleep* peacefully.

Didn't he always _read_ at night?	Yes, he always _read_ at night.
	No, he never _read_ at night.
Did he _not_ always _read_ at night?	Yes, he always _read_ at night.
	No, he never _read_ at night.

5. The second type of interrogative sentence is called a _wh- question_ because it is designed to elicit answers that provide content (information, facts, and so on) with a question word that begins with _wh-_ (except for _how_): _which, where, what, why, when, how_ (see Chapter 7). These words are normally put at the beginning of the sentence.

Question	Possible response
Which car do you prefer?	I prefer the Ford Mustang.
How's it going?	Quite well, thanks.
Where did he go yesterday?	He went to the movies.
What is that?	It's a new puzzle.
Why aren't you going?	Because I'm tired.
When are they coming?	Soon.

6. Questions can also be designed to seek approval, clarification, confirmation, consent, or agreement. These are called _tag questions_ because they are constructed with _isn't it? does she?_ and other similar "tags" added to the end of the sentence. These will be discussed further in Chapter 7. Note that if you wish to elicit an affirmative answer, use an affirmative sentence with a negative tag; however, if you wish to elicit a negative answer, use a negative sentence with an affirmative tag:

Affirmative sentence + negative tag	=	**Affirmative response**
John is British, _isn't he?_		Yes, he is.
Your mother drives a sports car, _doesn't she?_		Yes, she does.
She used to work there, _didn't she?_		Yes, she did.
You're coming too, _aren't you?_		Yes, I am.

Negative sentence + affirmative tag =	negative response
John isn't British, _is he?_	_No, he isn't._
Your mother does not drive a sports car, _does she?_	_No, she doesn't._
She did not use to work there, _did she?_	_No, she didn't._
You're not coming too, _are you?_	_No, I am not._

Exercise Set 1-4

A. Provide a question that elicits each answer.

1. I'm feeling well, thank you.
2. He's not going because he is very busy.
3. Yes, Alex is my brother.
4. No, her friends are not coming to the party.
5. Yes, I can do it.
6. Yes, he watches TV every night.
7. No, she does not like that sitcom.
8. They are arriving tomorrow around noon.
9. I prefer the house with three bedrooms.
10. They went to a disco last night.
11. I'm not sure what it is.
12. Yes, he did eat all of it.

B. Which response, (a) or (b), is the appropriate one?

1. He's coming too, isn't he?
   (a) Yes, he is.
   (b) No, he is coming.

2. She isn't coming, is she?
   (a) Yes, she is.
   (b) No, she isn't.

3. Your sister speaks Spanish, doesn't she?
   (a) Yes, she speaks.
   (b) Yes, she does.

4. Didn't you do it already?
   (a) Yes, I'm doing it.
   (b) Yes, I did.

5. Weren't they supposed to come?
   (a) Yes, they were.
   (b) Yes, they did suppose.

6. Were you looking for me?
   (a) Yes, I was.
   (b) Yes, I looked.

Clauses and Phrases

1. A simple sentence has only one subject and one predicate. Another way to characterize such a sentence is to say that it has one *clause*, known as an *independent clause*. As mentioned above, an independent clause is a properly formed combination of words consisting of a subject and a predicate that can stand alone:

Subject	**+**	**predicate**
Alexander		*is intelligent.*
My sister		*plays the piano.*

2. A complex sentence has at least one subordinate clause added to the independent (or main) clause. A subordinate clause cannot stand alone as a separate sentence because its meaning depends on the meaning of the main clause, about which it gives additional information. For this reason, it is called a *dependent clause*:

The girl	*who is reading the newspaper*	*is French.*
↑	↑	↑
main subject	dependent clause	main predicate

3. There are three types of dependent clauses, which will be discussed in Chapter 15. For now, note that they are called *adjective, noun,* and *adverb*.

4. An *adjective clause* (also called a *relative clause*) works like an adjective and is introduced by a relative pronoun (*that, which, who, whom,* and so on). It generally follows the subject or object that it describes:

    <u>who</u> is used when the subject or object refers to persons:

    The girl <u>who is reading the newspaper</u> is Italian.

    <u>that</u> / <u>which</u> is used when the subject or object refers to things:

    I love the book <u>that you are reading</u>.
    My house, <u>which is small and old</u>, is still home to me.

    <u>whose</u> is used to indicate possession:

    I met a girl <u>whose mother is a music teacher</u>.

5. A *noun clause* works like a noun and can thus function as the subject or object in a sentence. It is introduced (usually) by *that*.

    As subject:

    <u>That you came late</u> makes me angry.

    If the subject noun clause is put at the end of the sentence, then the expletive subject *it* is required:

    It makes me angry <u>that you came late</u>.

    As object:

    I know <u>that you are coming</u>.

6. An *adverb clause* functions like an adverb. It is introduced by a variety of conjunctions (*when, after, as soon as, while, because,* and so on). It can be put before or after the main clause. If put before, a comma must be used:

    <u>When Jack arrives</u>, we will go to the store.
    <u>After you left</u>, Sandra arrived.
    We arrived <u>as soon as you left</u>.
    <u>While you were sleeping</u>, I read the newspaper.

7. Compound sentences are formed by joining two independent clauses with a conjunction. In most cases, a comma is used between the first independent clause and the second. This is a rule of thumb, not an obligatory rule:

and signals an addition or connection of equal importance:

_Right now, Mary is studying _and_ her brother is watching TV._
The girl who has blonde hair and who speaks German quite well is American.

but / yet signals a contrast:

_Jenny wants to go, _but_ I do not._

_or_ signals choice:

_Claudia is sick, _or_ she is a good actor._

_so_ signals a result:

_Mary is not well, _so_ she is not going to work today._

for signals a reason:

_Alex is tired, _for_ he did not sleep very well last night._

8. These conjunctions can also be used to join individual words and phrases, not just clauses. In such cases a comma is not used:

_Mark _and_ Mary speak Chinese._
_I'm coming either with the car _or_ on foot._
_My grandson will study law _or_ medicine._

9. Another formula for creating compound sentences is the following one:

Mary isn't well;	_therefore_	_she's not going to work today._
↑	↑	↑
independent clause followed by a semicolon (;)	conjunctive adverb	independent clause

10. A *phrase* is a combination of words intended to add detail to a sentence.

   We waited <u>for hours</u>.
   My job is <u>to teach</u> English.

11. Notice that a clause has a subject and a verb. A phrase does not:

   Phrase: *We're going <u>to the opera</u>.*
   Clause: *We're going to the opera <u>so that we can enjoy ourselves</u>.*

12. The three main types of phrases are prepositional, gerund, and infinitive. A *prepositional phrase* begins with a preposition and contains a noun possibly with modifiers:

   I want to go <u>to the opera</u>.
   She lives <u>in the country</u>.

13. A *gerund* or *participial phrase*, as its name implies, begins with a gerund (a verb ending in *-ing*). It is always used as a substantive:

   <u>Reading comics</u> can be fun.
   There is great value in <u>living simply</u>.

14. An *infinitive phrase* begins with an infinitive:

   She brought a book <u>to lend me</u>.
   We'll have to hurry <u>to catch the plane</u>.

Exercise Set 1-5

A.   Correct the erroneous part in each sentence.

1. The person lives next to you is my cousin.
2. Did you go the movies last night?
3. Juan, Francesca speak Japanese.
4. I adore the book who I am reading right now.
5. Makes me happy that he calls all the time.
6. While he sleeps I usually read.
7. Watch movies is a great way to spend an evening together.

B.   Complete each sentence, choosing (a) or (b):

1. You'll have to run _____ .
    (a) to catch the bus.
    (b) catching the bus.

2. We're going the movies _____ .
    (a) so that that we can stay together for a while.
    (b) staying together for a while.

3. The boy _____ is a true genius.
    (a) which mother I know well
    (b) whose mother I know well

4. I'm going to the store _____ .
    (a) because I need milk.
    (b) I need milk.

5. He's going to the store _____ .
    (a) because he buys milk.
    (b) to buy milk.

6. He arrived _____ .
    (a) after we left.
    (b) that we left.

C.   Fill in each blank with an appropriate conjunction or relative pronoun.

1. The person _____ is talking is my good friend.
2. Mary _____ John should go to the party, but not both.
3. He got sick _____ he got a cold walking in the rain.
4. The book _____ you borrowed belongs to my sister.
5. He is not well, _____ he is going out just the same.
6. I like the house _____ you are building.

Typical Sentence Errors

1. A *dangling participle* is a participle (a verb form ending in *-ing*), usually in a subordinate clause, that lacks a clear grammatical relation with the subject of the sentence. It is best to avoid this construction because it forces the listener or reader to take a moment to determine the meaning of the sentence:

   Approaching New York, the skyline came into view.
   At age six, my mother taught me to play the piano.

   Better:

   As we approached New York, the skyline came into view.
   When I was six, my mother taught me to play the piano.

2. A *split infinitive* is an infinitive verb form with an element, usually an adverb, interposed between *to* and the verb:

   To boldly go where no one else has gone.
   We want to better serve you.

   Better:

   To go boldly where no one else has gone.
   We want to serve you better.

3. A *run-on sentence* is a sentence in which two or more independent clauses are improperly joined:

   It was a pleasant trip the sun was shining.
   They are siblings they may not look alike.

   Change to:

   It was a pleasant trip because the sun was shining.
   They are siblings, even though they may not look alike.

4. A *comma splice* is the improper use of a comma to join two independent clauses:

   It was a pleasant trip, the sun was shining.

Change to:

It was a pleasant trip because the sun was shining.

Or use a semicolon or a period:

It was a pleasant trip; the sun was shining.
It was a pleasant trip. The sun was shining.

Exercise Set 1-6

A. Correct each of the following sentences.

1. We drove all day, it was raining heavily.
2. They are still friends, they argue a lot.
3. It is a nice day, the sun is shining.
4. I am her brother, I do not look like her.

B. Choose the appropriate answer, (a) or (b):

1. Which sentence contains a dangling participle?
   (a) Leaving Chicago, the shoreline of Lake Michigan came into view.
   (b) As I was leaving Chicago, the shoreline of Lake Michigan came into view.

2. One of these sentences is preferable because it does not contain a dangling participle. Which one is it?
   (a) At age seven, my mom taught me to play the piano.
   (b) When I reached the age of seven, my mom taught me to play the piano.

3. Which sentence contains a split infinitive?
   (a) I want you to quickly do it.
   (b) I want you to do it quickly.

4. One of these sentences is preferable because it does not contain a split infinitive. Which one is it?
   (a) He likes to go to the movies often.
   (b) He like to often go to the movies.

2

Nouns

Grammar can govern even Kings.

Molière (1622–1673)

What Are Nouns?

1. *Nouns* are words that allow you to name and label the persons, entities, objects, places, and concepts that make up our world:

    That <u>boy</u> is tall.
    Those <u>girls</u> are also quite tall.

2. More specifically, they are names for

People:	*boy, girl, Alex, Sarah*
Places:	*New York, Chicago, home, school*
Animals:	*dog, cat, beetle, lion*
Things:	*car, book, radio, computer*
Things in nature:	*tree, flower, river, cliff*
Groups:	*bunch, crowd, herd*
Concepts:	*love, friendliness, happiness, joy*
Mass quantities:	*cheese, coffee, milk, dust*
Time designations:	*Monday, September, year, day*
Holidays:	*Christmas, Rosh Hashanah, Thanksgiving*
Nationalities:	*American, Mexican, Italian, French*

3. An adjective, a verb, a phrase, or a clause functioning as a subject or object in place of a noun is called a *substantive* or a *nominal*:

    <u>Swimming</u> is a healthy activity.
    <u>Eating</u> in moderation is key to a healthy life.
    <u>The rich</u> are spoiled.
    <u>To forget</u> is human.
    <u>Your coming late</u> makes me angry.

4. Nouns are classified as proper or common. *Proper* nouns are the names given to specific people, places, time units, nationalities, religions, languages, inhabitants, holidays, institutions, brand names, trademarks, and hurricanes. They are always capitalized, no matter where they occur in a sentence:

People and titles:

Mr. Redfern is a pleasant man.
Mary is a happy woman.
Professor Smith is a good friend.

Places and geographical names:

Jamaica is a beautiful island.
They live in Milwaukee.
Have you ever seen the Mississippi River?

Nationalities, religions, languages, inhabitants, and holidays:

He is Danish, not Irish.
They practice Buddhism.
I do not speak English very well.
Christmas is my favorite time of the year.
He is Catholic, isn't he?
Isn't French a beautiful language?
There are lots of Spaniards in that city.

Institutions:

He teaches at the University of Wisconsin.
The president lives in the White House.

The days of the week and the months:

They were both born in September.
We always go to the mall on Saturdays.

Brand names and trademarks:

He drives only <u>Fords</u>.
I do not like <u>Pepsi</u>; I prefer <u>Coke</u>.

Hurricanes:

<u>Hurricane Charlie</u> caused havoc along the coast.

5. Some proper nouns have only a plural form because they refer to plural entities. These require the definite article. So too do proper nouns referring to rivers, canals, oceans, mountains, universities, libraries, and other similar things:

the Virgin Islands
the United States
the Baltics
the Alps
the Atlantic Ocean
the Mississippi River
the Panama Canal
the University of Milwaukee
the Library of Congress
the Smithsonian
the Museum of Civilization

6. If the name of a university or similar institution does not include *of*, then the article is not used. This rule also applies in a few other cases:

Western Washington University
San Francisco Bay versus the Bay of Bengal

7. All other kinds of nouns are called *common*. They are the names given to kinds of people, places, things, and so on. Common nouns are not capitalized unless they occur at the beginning of a sentence.

That <u>man</u> is a pleasant person.
My <u>sister</u> is a happy person.
Their <u>house</u> is beautiful.

8. Common nouns are subdivided into count and noncount. *Count nouns* refer to anything that can be counted (*one book, two books,* and so on). They can be specified with any article, numeral, or quantity term (*many, several*) and have both a singular and a plural form.

Singular	**Plural**
a book	*four books*
one cake	*many cakes*
the church	*several churches*

9. *Noncount nouns*—also known as *mass nouns*—are words such as *sand, oil,* and *honesty* that denote anything that cannot be counted (at least by the speakers of the language). Such nouns can be specified by indefinite quantity terms such as *some* and *much,* but not by the indefinite article (*a / an*):

   some sand
   little honesty
   much oil
   some water
   a bit of sugar
   all the bread

10. Some noncount nouns can be used in a figurative sense. In such cases they are treated like count nouns:

    the waters of the Mediterranean Sea
    the sands of the Arabian Desert

Noncount Nouns

Noncount nouns can be classified into categories according to meaning. Here are some of them.

Nouns referring to groups of people, animals, entities, things:

clothing, baggage, band, class, family, food, furniture, garbage, hardware, jewelry, junk, luggage, mail, money, cash, change, traffic

Nouns referring to liquids, physical matter, and substances:

water, coffee, tea, milk, oil, sugar, soup, gasoline, ice, bread, butter, cheese, meat, gold, iron, silver, glass, paper, wood, cotton, wool, rice, chalk, corn, dirt, dust, flour, air, oxygen, smoke, smog

Nouns referring to abstractions and natural phenomena:

beauty, information, courage, education, fun, happiness, health, honesty, truth, time, space, work, weather, electricity

Nouns referring to fields of study, the arts, and so on:

literature, biology, philosophy, music mathematics, anthropology, geometry, ballet, religion

Nouns referring to recreation and sports:

baseball, soccer, chess, bridge, bowling, hiking

11. Noncount nouns referring to substances (food, liquid, and so on) can be put in the plural if a "variance" of the substance described is involved:

How many cheeses (kinds of cheese) would you like?
Would you like two or three sugars (lumps of sugar)?

12. Beverages can also be in the plural when referring to the container they are served in:

I had two bottles of beer.	or	*I had two beers.*
I had two kinds of beer.	or	*I had two beers.*

13. Noncount nouns referring to abstractions, natural phenomena, fields of study, the arts, recreation, and sports should not be specified with the definite article *(the)*:

Baseball is my favorite sport.
Do you like soccer?
He has courage.
Space is the next frontier.

14. Some nouns are classified as both count and noncount, but the meaning is different:

Noncount	Count
She has brown hair.	*She has a single hair on her dress.*
Please let in some light.	*Turn off the lights, please.*
Time is running out.	*I went to Vancouver four times last year.*

15. Finally, note that English borrows nouns from other languages. These can easily be identified by their different structures. For example, the following nouns, which end in a vowel, are borrowed from the Italian language:

salami
pizza
zucchini
opera

Exercise Set 2-1

A. Correct the spelling or grammatical error (or errors) in each sentence.

1. Where is ms. jones going?
2. I love the tennis.
3. Did you go to University of Florida?
4. She speaks the english very well, even though she is not american.
5. Have you ever met dr. Smith? Isn't he jewish?
6. I go downtown every saturday with my friends.
7. Aren't you of the russian origin?

B. Choose the noun that correctly completes each sentence, (a) or (b).

1. Would you please cut my _____ very short? It is getting rather long.
   (a) hair
   (b) hairs

2. I found several _____ on your shirt.
   (a) hair
   (b) hairs

3. Would you like some _____ ?
   (a) cheese
   (b) cheeses

4. How many _____ would you like?
   (a) cheese
   (b) cheeses

5. Do you want some _____ ?
   (a) coffee
   (b) waters

6. How many _____ did you take with you?
   (a) pieces of luggage
   (b) luggages

C.   Classify each noun.

checkers, Sarah, car, tulip, Paris, the Mississippi, machismo, Idaho, air, the Rockies, salami, friend, soprano, America, Japan, zucchini, opera, spaghetti, coin, shoe, cash, fun, key, bike, chess, gold, mathematics, Cadillac, game, poem, Kentucky, blitz, ravioli, bread, pizza, rice, gusto, Alex, work, dog

Proper	Count	Noncount	Borrowed

Gender

1. In English, common nouns are not normally classified according to gender, as they are in many other languages. However, a few nouns referring to persons sometimes indicate that the person is male or female. The suffix -ess, for example, is sometimes used to refer to females engaged in a profession, activity, and so on:

Male

waiter
actor

Female

waitress
actress

2. However, it is the tendency in modern day usage to avoid such distinctions. A word such as *actor* is now used commonly to refer to any actor, regardless of gender. If the gender of the individual is to be distinguished, for practical purposes, then *male* and *female* are used as modifiers in apposition (next to) the noun:

Male	Female
male doctor	*female doctor*
male lawyer	*female lawyer*
male actor	*female actor*
male nurse	*female nurse*
male secretary	*female secretary*

3. Like other languages, English uses different words and proper names for males and females when the distinction is socially meaningful:

Female	Male
mother	*father*
sister	*brother*
daughter	*son*
grandmother	*grandfather*
aunt	*uncle*
girl	*boy*
woman	*man*

Female name	Male name
Geraldine	*Gerald*
Michele (of French origin)	*Michael*

4. English has adopted the suffix *-a* (used, for example, in Spanish and Italian) to name female individuals. This is a limited practice, however.

Male	Female
Robert	*Roberta*
George	*Georgia*

5. Titles are nouns preceding the names of persons to indicate their gender, office, rank, or profession:

Male	Female
Mr. Smith	*Mrs. Smith, Miss Smith, Ms. Smith*
Dr. (Doctor) Jones	*Dr. (Doctor) Jones*
Prof. (Professor) Fox	*Prof. (Professor) Fox*
Rev. (Reverend) Bailey	*Rev. (Reverend) Bailey*

6. *Mrs.* is used as a title to indicate a married or widowed woman, and *Miss* a girl or a single woman, if such a distinction is required in a given situation. *Ms.* is used as a title to indicate any woman, married or not. Today, many women prefer this title because they feel that information about their marital status is a private matter.

7. There are fewer titles in English than there are in many other languages, such as French, Spanish, and Italian, which have titles for the professions of lawyer, draftsperson, and accountant, among others.

Exercise Set 2-2

A. Provide the corresponding male or female form of the noun.

Male	Female
1. Gerald	1. _____
2. _____	2. sister
3. waiter	3. _____
4. _____	4. female professor
5. male friend	5. _____
6. _____	6. Roberta
7. dad	7. _____
8. _____	8. chairwoman
9. spokesman	9. _____
10. _____	10. Doctor
11. Mr.	11. _____

B. Choose the correct form.

1. Mark is my _____ .
    (a) father
    (b) mother

2. Her _____ goes to an all-girl's school.
    (a) son
    (b) daughter

3. Your grandson is a very tall _____ .
    (a) boy
    (b) girl

4. That _____ doesn't know what she is talking about.
    (a) man
    (b) woman

5. She's my _____ .
    (a) uncle
    (b) aunt

6. They decided to call their daughter _____ .
    (a) Michael
    (b) Michele

Number

1. A count noun can be *singular* (referring to one person, thing, and so on) or *plural* (referring to more than one). This is called *number*. Noncount nouns, as mentioned above, have only a singular form (with a few exceptions):

honesty	but not	*honesties*
hunger	but not	*hungers*
chess	but not	*chesses*
furniture	but not	*furnitures*

2. Some nouns have only a plural form. They refer to things made up of more than one part:

scissors
pajamas
pants
jeans
shorts
spectacles (glasses)

> ### Pronunciation of *-s* / *-es*
>
> If the preceding sound is "voiceless" (*k,* *p, t, f, ...*), the *-s* ending is also voiceless:
>
> *cats = cat + s*
>
> If the preceding sound is "voiced" (*g, b,* *z, v, ...*), the *-s* ending is also pronounced voiced:
>
> *dogs = dog + z*
>
> In the case of *-es*, the *-e* is an indistinct vowel and the *-s* is pronounced voiced:
>
> *churches = church + ez*

3. To make a count noun ending in any vowel or consonant—except *-s,* *-z, -sh, -ch, -ge,* or *-x*—plural, simply add *-s* to the end of the noun:

Singular	Plural
auto	*autos*
memo	*memos*
boy	*boys*
friend	*friends*
game	*games*
girl	*girls*
lip	*lips*
uncle	*uncles*
judge	*judges*

4. If the noun ends in *-s, -z, -sh, -ch,* or *-x,* add *-es* instead:

Singular	Plural
church	*churches*
glass	*glasses*
peach	*peaches*
bush	*bushes*
sandwich	*sandwiches*
switch	*switches*
box	*boxes*

5. Some nouns ending in -o are changed to -es in the plural. But this is not the -es ending above. It is the result of a spelling change, not a phonetic one. It is pronounced as a single voiced sound:

Singular	Plural
tomato	tomatoes
potato	potatoes
echo	echoes
hero	heroes

> ### Sounds
>
> A *vowel* is produced by expelling the breath through the mouth with little or no obstruction.
>
> Vowels are represented by the letters a, e, i, o, u, and sometimes y, in the English alphabet.
>
> A *diphthong* begins with one vowel and gradually changes to another vowel within the same syllable:
> > boil
> > veil
>
> A consonant is produced by partial or complete obstruction of the breath.
>
> Consonants are represented by the remaining letters in the English alphabet: b, c, d, f, g, ...

6. If the noun ends in -y and is preceded by a vowel, simply add -s:

Singular	Plural
boy	boys
toy	toys

7. However, if the noun is preceded by a consonant, the ending is spelled -ies (although it is pronounced the same):

Singular	Plural
baby	babies
spy	spies
cherry	cherries
pharmacy	pharmacies

8. The endings of nouns ending in -f or -fe are changed to -ves. However, there are a number of exceptions to this rule. There is no absolute way to determine when to use -ves. You will simply have to check a dictionary:

Singular	Plural
-f or -fe	-ves
leaf	leaves
life	lives
knife	knives
loaf	loaves

half	*halves*
scarf	*scarves*
wolf	*wolves*
self	*selves*
shelf	*shelves*
thief	*thieves*

but

-f	*-fs*
belief	*beliefs*
roof	*roofs*
chief	*chiefs*
cliff	*cliffs*

9. Some nouns have the same singular and plural forms:

Singular	**Plural**
one deer	*many deer*
one species	*two species*
one sheep	*four sheep*
one series	*several series*

10. Be careful! The noun *people* is singular in form but plural in meaning and thus requires a plural verb in clauses and sentences:

   <u>People</u> <u>speak</u> too much.
   I have always thought that most <u>people</u> <u>speak</u> too much.

11. Nouns ending in *-sis* in the singular are of Greek origin. In the plural they are changed to *-ses:*

Singular	**Plural**
crisis	*crises*
hypothesis	*hypotheses*
thesis	*theses*
analysis	*analyses*
parenthesis	*parentheses*
oasis	*oases*

12. Nouns ending in -*um* and -*us* are of Latin origin. In the plural they are changed, respectively, to -*a* and -*i*:

Singular	Plural
memorandum	*memoranda*
datum	*data*
compendium	*compendia*
medium	*media*
radius	*radii*
nucleus	*nuclei*
stimulus	*stimuli*

13. Also of foreign origin are the following:

Singular	Plural
appendix	*appendices*
criterion	*criteria*
cactus	*cacti*
phenomenon	*phenomena*

14. Some nouns are irregular, that is, they do not have plural forms consistent with any of the above rules. You will simple have to learn these as you go along:

Singular	Plural
child	*children*
foot	*feet*
man	*men*
mouse	*mice*
ox	*oxen*
woman	*women*
tooth	*teeth*

Exercise Set 2-3

A. Make the following nouns plural.

1. baby
2. potato
3. hero
4. desk
5. branch
6. toy
7. chief
8. attorney
9. roof
10. life
11. knife
12. bridge

B. You are given the plural forms of the following nouns. Provide their singular forms.

1. teeth
2. mice
3. phenomena
4. children
5. oxen
6. species
7. feet
8. leaves
9. cacti
10. indices
11. stimuli
12. radii
13. media
14. analyses
15. theses

C. Correct the following.

1. sheeps
2. deers
3. nucleuses
4. dormitorys
5. shelfs
6. halfs
7. loafs
8. scarfs
9. spys
10. cherrys
11. traffics
12. patiences
13. scissor
14. pant
15. pharmacys

Nouns as Modifiers

1. Nouns can be used as modifiers of other nouns:

    vegetable soup   a soup made with vegetables
    office building   a building that has offices in it

2. When a noun modifier is combined with a numerical expression, it must be in the singular and a hyphen must be used to connect the parts:

    two-hour test   a test that lasts two hours
    four-year-old brother a brother who is four years old

3. If possession is intended, simply add 's if the noun is singular. This type of noun modifier is called, logically, a *possessive noun*:

    the boy's book   the book that belongs to the boy
    Mary's husband   the husband married to Mary

4. Add 's even to singular nouns that themselves end in *-s*. In this case, you can also add just an apostrophe instead:

    Dickens's novel   or   *Dickens' novel*
    the witness's story   or   *the witness' story*

5. Add an apostrophe if the noun is plural and ends in -s; otherwise add 's:

    the boys' books
    the ladies' books

    but

    the children's game
    women's liberation

6. Because gerunds can function as nouns, possessive nouns can also be used to modify gerunds:

    He complained about Mary's coming to class late.
    We always worry about the professor's running absent-mindedly from class to class.

7. When one of the nouns in a series is a possessive, all the others in the series must also be possessive:

    Bill's, Mark's, and Jenny's friends
    the boys' and girls' teams

8. A noun or noun phrase placed next to another as an explanatory equivalent is said to be in *apposition*: for example, *Brent* and *the painter* in *The painter Brent was born in Boston* are nouns in apposition.

Exercise Set 2-4

A. Provide the correct form of the possessive noun or noun phrase:

    Example: the farmer market
              the farmer's market

    1. a dollar worth
    2. the book success
    3. my brother, sister, and friend favorite movie
    4. five week pay
    5. the fox cunning
    6. the vegetable drink
    7. the office party

8. Jean friend
9. the girl dress
10. New Year Day
11. several three minute exercise
12. my twenty year old cousin

B.   Change each to the plural.

Example: the boy's friends
the boys' friends

1. the girl's friends
2. the mother's routine
3. the witness's story
4. the man's washroom
5. the child's puzzle
6. the leaf's color

Affixes

1. An *affix* is a form attached to a core (indivisible) word, known as a *root*. For example, the word *unmanly* has one root *(man)* and two affixes, one attached at the front and one at the end. The former is called a *prefix*, and the latter a *suffix:*

<u>*unmanly*</u>   unbecoming to a man

2. Affixes can be used with most parts of speech, not just nouns. In the first example below, the root is an adjective, and in the second it is a verb

Root	**Prefix**	**Suffix**
complete	*incomplete*	*completely*
believe	*disbelieve*	*believable*

3. Affixes add nuances or elements of meaning to root words:

Root	**+**	**Suffix**	
child		*childish*	lack of maturity
trend		*trendy*	in style

4. Here are some common noun suffixes:

Suffix	Meaning	Examples
-er	carries out an activity	*teacher, lawyer, player*
-or	trained in an activity or charged with a duty	*doctor, mayor, actor*
-ee	acted on / recipient of an action	*employee, retiree*
-ion	process, activity, act	*reduction, admission*
-ism	belief, ideology, profession	*liberalism, journalism*
-ness	an abstract quality of something	*goodness, happiness*

Exercise Set 2-5

A. For each of the following words identify the root and the affix.

1. illegal
2. friendly
3. unfriendly
4. miscalculation
5. disbelief
6. believable
7. recoverable

B. Choose (a) or (b) as the case may be.

1. He hired several _____ .
   (a) employers
   (b) employees

2. For _____ sake, why did you not call me earlier?
   (a) goodness'
   (b) liberalism

3. He is a wonderful _____ . I have learned everything I know from him.
   (a) teacher
   (b) doctor

4. Who is your _____ ?
   (a) lawyer
   (b) jurisdiction

5. She always wears _____ clothes.
   (a) stylish
   (b) trendiest

Compound Nouns

1. *Compound nouns* are nouns that are made up of two parts:

   <u>hand</u> <u>kerchief</u>   <u>take</u> <u>over</u>
   ↑   ↑   ↑   ↑
   noun + noun   verb + preposition

2. Here are some examples:

Noun + noun	Adjective + noun	Noun + phrase or phrase + noun	Verb + noun or noun + verb	Preposition + noun	Verb + preposition
birdbath	blackberry	mother-in-law	managing editor	downpour	cleanup
bookstore	common sense	editor-in-chief	problem solving	online	walkout
credit card	blueberry	brother-in-law	answering machine	in-depth	makeup
baseball	brownfield	for-profit scheme	binge eating	in-flight	call-up

3. As you can see, many compound nouns are written as single words. However, some are written as separate words or as hyphenated words:

   As single words

   railroad
   necklace
   screwdriver
   headache
   notebook
   walkout
   crackdown
   input
   output

As separate words

science fiction
credit card
answering machine

As hyphenated words

cut-rate
built-up

4. To form the plurals of compound nouns, follow the same rules as those for simple nouns:

Singular	**Plural**
railroad	*railroads*
credit card	*credit cards*
newlywed	*newlyweds*
blueberry	*blueberries*

5. The exception is the *noun + hyphenated phrase* compound form, in which the noun is pluralized:

Singular	**Plural**
mother-in-law	*mothers-in-law*
editor-in-chief	*editors-in-chief*

6. Of course, noncount compound nouns have only a singular form:

birth control
family planning
pocket money
greenhouse effect

7. Some compound nouns have only a plural form if they refer to things made up of more than one part:

grass roots
sunglasses
race relations

Exercise Set 2-6

A. Identify the two parts of each compound noun.

1. greenhouse
2. family planning
3. birth control
4. sunglasses
5. makeup
6. answering machine
7. input
8. walkout
9. screwdriver

B. Put the following compound nouns into their plural forms.

1. headache
2. notebook
3. output
4. railroad
5. managing editor
6. bookstore
7. sister-in-law

3

Determiners

Grammar is the logic of speech, even as logic is the grammar of reason.

Richard Chevenix Trench (1807–1886)

What Are Determiners?

1. *Determiners* are words placed before nouns or noun phrases, specifying them in some way. *Articles*, for instance, are determiners that signal whether the item to which a noun refers is specific (*the book on the table*) or nonspecific (*a book in general*). The former type of article is called *definite*, and the latter *indefinite*:

Specific **(definite article)**	**Nonspecific** **(indefinite article)**
the book	*a book*
the girl	*a girl*

2. *Demonstratives* and *possessives* are classified as determiners in this book, although you might find them listed as adjectives in other reference grammars. They are classified as determiners here because they too have a specifying function—demonstratives specify whether someone or something is relatively near or far, and possessives specify to whom or to what something belongs:

this book	*that book*
my book	*your book*

> **A Rule of Thumb**
>
> As a rule of thumb, the indefinite article is used when the noun refers to something in general. No article is used in the plural:
>
> *An apple a day is good for you.*
> *Apples are good for you.*
>
> The indefinite article is also used when the noun refers to something nonspecific. A quantity term, such as *some*, is used in the plural:
>
> *I'll have an apple.*
> *I usually have some apples with me.*
>
> The definite article is used instead when the noun (singular or plural) refers to something specific or definite:
>
> *Thanks for the apple.*
> *I bought the apples, not the oranges.*

44

3. Quantity terms and expressions such as *any*, *both*, *a lot of*, and *some* are also classified as determiners. These are known generally as *quantifiers*.

Exercise Set 3-1

A.   Identify each determiner.

1. the orange
2. an orange
3. some oranges
4. this book
5. your books
6. any movie
7. several tickets

B. Choose the appropriate determiner.

1. I need _____ new car.
   (a) a
   (b) the

2. I want _____ car, not that one.
   (a) the
   (b) this

3. I'll have _____ fruit drink of any kind.
   (a) a
   (b) the

4. I'll have _____ fruit drink you had yesterday.
   (a) a
   (b) the

5. _____ fruit drinks are good for you.
   (a) Those
   (b) Your

6. _____ fruit drinks are better than others.
(a) The
(b) Some

Articles

1. There are two distinct forms of the indefinite article: (1) *a* before a consonant or *u* pronounced as "yooh"; and (2) *an* before a vowel or "silent *h*" (*h* that is not pronounced):

Before a consonant	Before a vowel
a boy	*an egg*
a friend	*an angel*
a hat	*an honor* (*h* is silent)
a union (*u* = "yooh")	*an umbrella*

2. Be careful! When an adjective or some other part of speech precedes a noun, you have to adjust the article according to its initial sound:

a boy	*an intelligent boy*	not	*a intelligent boy*
a friend	*an old friend*	not	*a old friend*

3. The indefinite article is never used with noncount nouns or plural count nouns:

Count nouns	Noncount nouns
a boy	*some water / a bit of water*
a friend	*some rice / a bit of rice*

Plural count nouns	
oranges	*some oranges*
tables	*some tables*

4. The indefinite article is used with a noun referring to something in general; in this case it means "any" without specification:

I want an orange.	or	*I want any orange in general.*
I need a pencil.	or	*I need any pencil, no matter what kind.*

5. Finally, the indefinite article is used in exclamations starting with *What*:

   What a great movie that was!
   What a beautiful dress you are wearing!

6. There is one form of the definite article in standard American English: *the*. It is pronounced differently in most parts of the United States depending on whether it occurs before a consonant or before a vowel. Before a consonant its final vowel is pronounced as an indistinct sound similar to the sound "uh"; before a vowel it is pronounced as a sound similar to "eeh":

Before a consonant ("uh")	Before a vowel ("eeh")
the boy	*the egg*
the friend	*the angel*

7. The definite article is used to specify the noun in some way:

Count nouns	Noncount nouns
the boy	*the water*
the friend	*the rice*

8. It is thus used when…

   the noun is known to the speaker:

   The car I bought is very expensive.
   The answer we are looking for is not easy to find.

   the noun is unique and specific:

   The sun rises in the east.
   The moon is a silver color tonight.

   the noun is representative of a general class:

   The car is putting everybody's health at risk.
   The cello is a great instrument.

9. When a professional title is followed by a person's name, or when a title is used while talking to a person directly, the article is dropped:

The doctor is in today.
The professor teaches art.

but

Dr. Valdez is in today.
Prof. Jones teaches art.

"Doctor, are you in?"
"Professor, do you teach art?"

10. The definite article also is not used

with nouns expressing general ideas:

Water is a liquid.
We need water to survive.
Food is necessary to live.
Oliver likes Chinese food.
Patience is a virtue.
Please try to have more patience.
Americans are nice.
Books help us understand.
We all need books to help us understand.

with proper geographical names (continents, countries, states, cities, islands, and mountains) unless the names are plural or unless they refer to bodies of water:

Italy	*the United States*
Alabama	*the Philippines*
Central America	*the Tiber River*
Everest	*the Alps*
Mexico	*the Pacific Ocean*

with bays, harbors, ports, and so on, that are named, unless the name follows:

San Francisco Bay	**but**	*the Bay of Fundy*
New York Harbor	**but**	*the Port Authority*

with dates:

1492 is an important year in the history of America.
Today is November third.

with names of languages and school subjects:

We are learning Spanish.   *Spanish is a nice language.*
I am studying mathematics.   *Mathematics is not that hard to*
                                                understand.

11. With the number of a day in a month the definite article is optional
    in the first example below, but obligatory in the second example:

    Today is November third   **or**   *Today is November the third*
                                                    (optional)
    Today is November third   **or**   *Today is the third of November*
                                                    (obligatory)

12. Normally, the definite article is dropped with nouns in prepositional
    phrases starting with *to* and *at* and indicating an unspecified place or
    location. This is just a rule of thumb, and there are exceptions to it:

    Retained   **Dropped**

    He goes to the same school   *He goes to school often.*
      John attends?
    Welcome to the home of   *They are always at home.*
      the Smiths.
    They go to the movies often.   *They go to church often.*
    They are at the library.

13. Finally, notice that the same article forms do not need to be repeated
    before every noun or noun phrase:

    a boy and a girl   **or**   *a boy and girl*
    the young boy and the young girl   **or**   *the young boy and girl*

Exercise Set 3-2

A. Put the correct form of the indefinite article in front of the following nouns.

Example: boy
   a boy

1. girl
2. intelligent girl
3. man
4. American woman
5. house
6. hour
7. late hour
8. underdog

B. Use the correct form of the definite or the indefinite article, as the case may be. Note that an article may not be required.

1. I would love _____ piece of chocolate cake, no matter what kind it is.
2. I would love _____ rice that you made yesterday.
3. I need _____ new TV set.
4. _____ TV set you bought yesterday is a plasma set, isn't it?
5. What _____ great deal that was!
6. I need _____ new shoes.
7. _____ rice is good for you, generally speaking.
8. _____ rice is tastier than the pasta.
9. Do you know _____ doctor who lives next door to us?
10. "Good morning, _____ Doctor Banning."
11. _____ Doctor Smith lives next door to us.
12. _____ books I gave you yesterday are very good.
13. _____ books are important learning tools.
14. I love _____ Italian food.
15. Do you play _____ piano?
16. Have you ever been to _____ Germany?
17. No, but I have been to _____ Philippines.
18. Have you ever seen _____ San Francisco Bay?

19. Today is September _____ fifteenth.
20. Today is _____ twenty-first of September.
21. I love studying _____ geometry.
22. Are you going to _____ movies tonight?
23. I often go to _____ church on Sundays.

Demonstratives

1. *Demonstratives* are determiners that allow you to indicate if someone or something is relatively near or far.

Relatively near

Singular	**Plural**
this	*these*
this chair	*these chairs*
this newspaper	*these newspapers*
this exercise	*these exercises*
this room	*these rooms*
this hour	*these hours*

Relatively far

Singular	**Plural**
that	*those*
that chair	*those chairs*
that newspaper	*those newspapers*
that exercise	*those exercises*
that room	*those rooms*
that hour	*those hours*

2. The same demonstrative forms sometimes need not be repeated before every noun or noun phrase.

this boy and this girl	or	*this boy and girl*
those young boys and those young girls	or	*those young boys and girls*

3. Demonstratives are rarely used with noncount nouns unless followed by a specifying phrase, clause, or other form. In this case their use is optional:

   I would like some of that sugar over there.
   I ate all of that rice because it was very good.

4. With nouns referring to various abstract notions, demonstratives often indicate "closeness" of a nonphysical nature. For example, the expression *this idea* indicates that the speaker is close to the idea (mentally); whereas *that idea* indicates that he or she is distant from it (mentally).

Exercise Set 3-3

A. Change into the singular or the plural form, as the case may be.

   1. that boy
   2. this woman
   3. these ideas
   4. those cars
   5. that argument
   6. these leaves
   7. this mistake

B. Supply the appropriate form of the demonstrative.

   1. _____ books over there belong to my sister.
   2. _____ books here belong to me.
   3. Who is _____ man walking on the other side of the street?
   4. I do not recognize _____ person right here in the photograph.
   5. I would like to eat all of _____ rice over there, but I am too full.
   6. I have made _____ same mistake over and over.
   7. I am distancing myself from _____ ideas, because they have become old-fashioned.

Possessives

1. Possessives are classified as determiners in this book because they indicate ownership of, or relationship to, what a noun or noun phrase represents. They can also be classified as adjectives:

   my book (ownership of)   the book belongs to me
   our friends (relationship to)   they are friends of ours

2. Possessives vary according to person (first, second, third), number (singular, plural), and, in the case of the third person singular, gender (masculine, feminine, neuter):

	Singular	**Plural**
first person	*my*	*our*
second person	*your*	*your*
third person (masculine)	*his*	*their*
third person (feminine)	*her*	*their*
third person (neuter)	*its*	*their*

3. Notice that the third person singular possessives *his* and *her* refer to individuals whose gender is known; *its* refers instead to a thing or an entity whose gender is not essential:

   That student, whose name is <u>John</u>, never hands in <u>his</u> assignments on time.
   That other student, whose name is <u>Mary</u>, always hands in <u>her</u> assignments on time.
   That <u>dog</u> is always licking <u>its</u> paws.

   ### *Its* Versus *It's*

   Its without the apostrophe is a possessive form:

   A bird uses its wings to fly.
   It has its own timing device.

   It's with the apostrophe is a contraction of *it is* or *it has*:

It is 10:30.	or	*It's 10:30.*
It is my book.	or	*It's my book.*
It has been a long time.	or	*It's been a long time.*

   ---

4. If the gender of a noun modified by a possessive adjective is not known, the generic form *his or her*, or even *their*, must be used:

   <u>Everyone</u> always hands in <u>his or her</u> assignment late.
   <u>Everyone</u> always hands in <u>their</u> assignments late.

5. If the possessive is preceded by an indefinite phrase (*a friend of, an uncle of*, and so on), the pronoun form must be used:

my uncle	versus	*an uncle of mine*	an unspecified uncle
his friend	versus	*a friend of his*	an unspecified friend

6. The pronoun forms of the possessive are as follows. These pronouns are discussed again in Chapter 5:

	Singular	**Plural**
first person	*mine*	*ours*
second person	*yours*	*yours*
third person (masculine)	*his*	*theirs*
third person (feminine)	*hers*	*theirs*
third person (neuter)	*its*	*theirs*

7. To emphasize ownership, *own* can be used after the possessive adjective:

I make <u>my own</u> clothes.
She has <u>her own</u> key.

Exercise Set 3-4

A. Complete each sentence with the appropriate possessive adjective.

1. Mary, where do you think you lost _____ purse?
2. Mary always hands in _____ assignments on time.
3. Mary's brother, on the other hand, always hands in _____ assignments late.
4. That dog is always licking _____ paws.
5. We are not sure if _____ parents will agree to let us go out tonight.
6. Where are those two people? They left _____ briefcases on the table.
7. Everyone should be thankful for _____ good fortune.

B. Choose the appropriate possessive form, (a) or (b).

1. Do you make _____ clothes?
   (a) yours
   (b) your own

2. She is a friend of _____ whom I haven't seen in a long time.
   (a) my
   (b) mine

3. Jenny, is that _____ ?
   (a) yours
   (b) its

4. Yesterday I met your brother who was out shopping with a friend of _____ .
   (a) hers
   (b) his

5. Everybody should look after _____ business first.
   (a) their own
   (b) its

6. She is an aunt of _____ ; we really love her.
   (a) ours
   (b) his or her

7. That clock has _____ own timing device.
   (a) its
   (b) it's

8. Don't go yet! _____ still quite early.
   (a) Its
   (b) It's

Quantifiers

1. *Quantifiers* are determiners indicating quantity (*some, all of, most, several,* and so on). The most common quantifiers are *some* and *a lot of.* When used with noncount nouns, they convey the idea of an unspecified quantity, with *some* indicating that the quantity is relatively small, and *a lot of / lots of* indicating it is relatively large:

Unspecified small quantity	Unspecified large quantity
some water	*a lot of / lots of water*
some sugar	*a lot of / lots of sugar*
some meat	*a lot of / lots of meat*
some wine	*a lot of / lots of wine*
some information	*a lot of / lots of information*
some bread	*a lot of / lots of bread*

2. The quantifiers *not any / no, plenty of, most of the, all the, a little, much,* and *a great deal of* are also used with noncount nouns to provide different degrees of quantitative detail

No quantity at all	Entire quantity
no water	*all the water*
no information	*all the information*

Small quantity	Greater quantity
a little water	*much water*
a little wine	*much wine*

Nearly all the quantity	A relatively large quantity
most of the bread	*plenty of / a great deal of bread*
most of the information	*plenty of / a great deal of information*

3. In colloquial English, *some* is often omitted before such nouns:

I want some meat.	or	*I want meat.*
I'm eating some spaghetti.	or	*I'm eating spaghetti.*

4. *Some* can also be used with nouns referring to abstract ideas, with the same kind of meaning:

    You must show some integrity.
    I have some idea why he didn't show up.

5. A *bit of* and *a little* are synonyms of *some* (with noncount nouns). The former is used when the noun refers to solid substances and gases, and the latter in reference to liquid substances:

    Solids / gases

some meat	*a bit of meat*
some sugar	*a bit of sugar*
some oxygen	*a bit of oxygen*

    Liquids

some water	*a little water*
some wine	*a little wine*

6. When used with count nouns, *some* functions essentially as the plural form of the indefinite article:

Singular	**Plural (an unspecified quantity)**
a / an	*some*
a book	*some books*
an apple	*some apples*

7. The quantifiers *several* and *a few* are used only with count nouns to indicate that something is of a number more than two or three, but not many:

Unspecified	**More than two or three, but not many**
some uncles	*several / a few uncles*
some glasses	*several / a few glasses*
some forks	*several / a few forks*
some friends	*several / a few friends*

8. *Some* can be used as well to indicate an indefinite additional quantity. It can also be used as an adverb to indicate approximation:

> *She did the assigned work and then some.*
> *Some forty people attended the rally.*

9. Quantifiers can be used with the preposition *of* to emphasize the type of quantity involved:

Agreement

In expressions of quantity constructed with *of* (*some of, a lot of,* and so on), the number of the verb is determined by the noun or pronoun that follows *of*:

> *Some of those <u>books</u> <u>are</u> new.*
> *A lot of the <u>equipment</u> <u>is</u> new.*

The exceptions to this rule are *one, every,* and *each*:

> *<u>One</u> of the CDs <u>is</u> mine.*
> *<u>Each</u> of those books <u>is</u> new.*

> *I want some of those books, but not all.*
> *I want some of that cake, but not all of it.*
> *I need some of the things you mentioned, but not every one of them.*
> *Many of my friends are here.*
> *Several of the students knew about it.*
> *All of them left early.*

10. *Whichever* and *whatever* are quantifiers that render the idea of something being any part of a group:

> *Read whichever books you please!*
> *It's a long trip whatever road you take.*

11. To make sentences composed of quantifiers negative, replace the relevant quantifier with *not ... any*.

Affirmative	**Negative**
I have <u>some</u> sugar.	*I <u>don't</u> have <u>any</u> sugar.*
I bought <u>a few</u> books.	*I <u>didn't</u> buy <u>any</u> books.*
There are <u>several</u> students here.	*There <u>aren't</u> <u>any</u> students here.*
She is eating <u>several</u> oranges.	*She <u>isn't</u> eating <u>any</u> oranges.*

12. An alternative way to make such sentences negative is simply to use *no* before the noun:

I don't have any sugar.	*I have no sugar.*
There aren't any students here.	*There are no students here.*

13. Other common quantity terms and expressions are as follows:

enough **(sufficient, adequate)**

I do not have enough money.

every **(all) + singular noun**

Every morning we read the newspaper.

each **(every, all) + singular noun**

In Louisville you can eat well in each downtown restaurant.

other **(additional, new, different)**

Who is the other girl?

certain **(particular)**

I know a certain gentleman named Robert.

a lot of **(many)**

Yesterday I ate a lot of sweets.

few **(not many)**

There are few female students in this class.

little **(not much)**

There is only a little of the cake left, but not much.

too much **(a large amount) + singular noun (expresses a negative idea)**

We ate too much ice cream yesterday (so we felt sick).

Overview

Used only with count nouns in the singular—*one, each, every*:

> *one apple*
> *each apple / every apple*

Used only with count nouns in the plural—*both, a couple of, a few, several, many, a number of*:

> *both shoes*
> *a couple of apples*
> *a few pears*
> *several oranges*
> *many friends*
> *a number of chores*

Used only with noncount nouns—*a little, much, a great deal of*

> *a little salt*
> *much patience*
> *a great deal of patience*

Used with both count and noncount nouns—*some, any, no, a lot of, a great deal of, lots of, plenty of, most, all*:

> *some water*   *some apples*
> *any milk*   *any friends*

too many (a large number) + plural noun (expresses a negative idea)

Too many tourists visit the White House every year (so it's hard to get a reservation).

quite (rather, reasonably)

This cake is quite good.

much (a great deal) + singular noun

There is much work to do here.

many (a great deal) + plural noun

There are many students in this class.

all (the entire amount)—separated from the noun by the definite article (and optionally followed by the preposition *of*):

She ate all the rice.   *She ate all of the rice.*
Miguel ate all the soup.   *Miguel ate all of the soup.*

Exercise Set 3-5

A.   Provide the correct quantifier or correct form of the verb (as the case may be).

1. I would like certain water, please.
2. May I have a little books?
3. He ate much of the cake, but not all of it.
4. We bought much books yesterday.
5. Some of those clothes is new.
6. Some of that equipment are new.
7. One of the books are mine.
8. Each of those DVDs are new.
9. I will never eat some meat again.
10. I do not have many money.
11. Some morning we read the newspaper.
12. I know that girl. But who is the certain girl?

B. Choose the appropriate answer, (a) or (b).

1. Yesterday he bought _____ bread.
   (a) a lot of
   (b) several

2. I want only _____ sugar.
   (a) all the
   (b) a little

3. I need _____ things, but not many.
   (a) several
   (b) a little

4. Incredibly, _____ ninety people came to the party.
   (a) some
   (b) plenty of

5. _____ of your friends came to the party, but not all.
   (a) Many
   (b) Every one

6. Go and see _____ movie you want, but avoid going to the movie theater in that mall.
   (a) whichever
   (b) some

7. I don't have _____ oranges.
   (a) some
   (b) any

8. There are _____ students in the classroom.
   (a) any
   (b) no

4

Adjectives and Adverbs

*In fact, words are well adapted for description and
the arousing of emotion, but for many kinds of precise
thought other symbols are much better.*

J. B. S. Haldane (1892–1964)

What Are Descriptive Adjectives?

1. *Descriptive adjectives* are words that modify or describe nouns; that is, they give further information about the noun. Adjectives are placed before the nouns they modify:

   It's a <u>new</u> house.
   That's a <u>good</u> book.

2. They can also be separated from the nouns they modify by a linking or a sense verb. A *linking verb* such as *be, seem, appear,* or *become* is one that links the adjective to the subject. A *sense verb* such as *taste, smell, feel, sound,* or *look* also links the adjective to the subject. Adjectives used in this way are known as *predicate adjectives* because they occur in the predicate slot, after the verb that links them to the nouns they modify.

   With linking verbs:

   The sweater and the purse <u>are</u> <u>red</u>.
   Sarah <u>is</u> very <u>kind</u>.
   Alex <u>is</u> <u>wonderful</u>.
   They <u>seem</u> very <u>generous</u>.
   This shirt <u>is becoming</u> <u>old</u>.

With sense verbs:

The milk tastes sour.
I feel sick.
That music sounds beautiful.
She looks gorgeous.

3. When other parts of speech are used to modify the noun, they must precede the adjective.

   He is a very pleasant boy.
   He is a pleasant and good boy.

4. Unlike other languages (for example, Spanish, French, and Italian), adjectives are invariable in English—that is, you can never pluralize them:

Singular	**Plural**		
the new church	*the new churches*	never	*the news churches*
the large leaf	*the large leaves*	never	*the larges leaves*
the tall woman	*the tall women*	never	*the talls women*
the easy word	*the easy words*	never	*the easies words*
the green plant	*the green plants*	never	*the greens plants*

5. The endings *-al*, *-ful*, *-able*, *-ible*, *-y*, *-less*, and *-ous* are often found on adjectives:

   They are typical teenagers.
   She is a wonderful person.
   That was an enjoyable meal.
   That food is not edible.
   They always wear trendy clothes.
   You're in a hopeless situation.
   Hers is a very generous offer.
   That is a marvelous book.

6. Descriptive adjectives specify qualities of the nouns they modify. They make up the largest group of adjectives. The other main types of adjectives are *possessive* and *interrogative*. However, in this book possessive adjectives have been treated in Chapter 3 as determiners. Interrogatives will be discussed in Chapter 7.

Exercise Set 4-1

A. The following adjectives are missing from the given sentences. Put them in the blanks according to meaning.

> beautiful, new, generous, easy, blue, sweet, tattered, intelligent, stunning, bright

1. I bought a brand _____ plasma TV set yesterday.
2. They are very _____ children.
3. The sweater and the purse are _____ .
4. Sarah is an _____ person who always scores high on IQ tests.
5. My grandson is a very _____ person who helps people in need.
6. That test might seem _____ , but it is actually quite difficult.
7. These shoes are becoming _____ .
8. The chocolates taste very _____ .
9. That symphony sounds _____ .
10. She looks _____ in that dress.

B. Do you know how to change each noun into an adjective?

Example: wonder
           wonderful

1. joy
2. critique / criticism
3. work
4. sense
5. cream
6. pleasure
7. penny

Adjectival Constructions

1. The present participle can be used as an adjective. Known as a *participial adjective*, it replaces verb clauses:

Verb clause	Participial adjective
the show that annoys me	*the <u>annoying</u> show*
a story that moves her	*a <u>moving</u> story*

2. A *compound adjective*, like a compound noun (see Chapter 2), is made up of two parts and is often written with a hyphen separating them:

good-natured	of a good nature
well-known	known by many
left-handed	uses the left hand
absent-minded	forgetful, distracted
self-centered	thinks only of himself or herself

3. Some compound adjectives are constructed with a preposition:

all-out effort	total effort
built-in furniture	furniture that cannot be easily removed
worn-out shoes	shoes that cannot be worn anymore

The Present Participle

For full details on how to form the present participle, go to the relevant section in Chapter 8.

For the present purposes, it is sufficient to know that, in general, the present participle is formed by simply putting the ending *-ing* on the infinitive (the dictionary form of the verb):

Infinitive	Present participle
play	*playing*
read	*reading*
listen	*listening*
sing	*singing*
live	*living*

Exercise Set 4-2

A. Give the appropriate participial adjective.

> Example: a show that annoys people
> *an annoying show*

  1. a nun who sings
  2. a device that allows one to listen
  3. a light that permits one to read clearly
  4. a field where one can play
  5. a friend who shows much love
  6. a gesture that shows that someone knows something
  7. a poem that moves one (to tears)

B.   Give the appropriate compound adjective.

> Example: clothes that cannot be worn any longer.
> *worn-out clothes*

  1. people who think only of themselves
  2. a politician known by many
  3. a distracted professor
  4. a device that cannot be removed
  5. a clinic into which one can walk and receive attention without an appointment
  6. people who have a good disposition or mood or show a good humor

What Are Adverbs?

  1. *Adverbs* are words that modify verbs, adjectives, or other adverbs. They convey meanings that involve relations of time, place, degree of intensity, and manner:

Mary <u>drives</u> <u>slowly</u>.

        ↑   ↑

     verb adverb

This house is very beautiful.

     ↑   ↑

  adverb adjective

John drives too slowly.

    ↑   ↑

  adverb   adverb

2. Essentially, adverbs answer questions such as the following:

How?	*She walks quickly.*
Where?	*She walks outside a lot.*
When?	*She walks daily.*
To what extent?	*She walks very fast.*

3. Adverbs of manner allow you to express how something occurs, unfolds, or is done. They are formed by adding the ending *-ly* to most corresponding adjectives or nouns:

love	*lovely*	in a manner that evokes love
slow	*slowly*	in a slow manner
certain	*certainly*	in a certain manner
clear	*clearly*	in a clear manner
true	*truly*	in a true manner or sense

4. If the noun or adjective ends in *-le*, this ending is itself changed to *-ly*:

simple	*simply*
able	*ably*

5. If the noun or adjective ends in *-y*, the *-y* is rewritten as *-i*:

easy	*easily*
lucky	*luckily*
happy	*happily*

6. If the noun or adjective ends in a vowel + *-l*, the *-l* is written as a double letter:

useful	*usefully*
special	*specially*

7. Adverbs of manner normally follow the verb but may begin a sentence for emphasis.

> *He sends his friends e-mails regularly. / Regularly, he sends his friends e-mails.*

8. As mentioned, adverbs and adverbial phrases of all kinds are needed for various purposes—to specify time, to indicate location, and so on. Some very useful ones are provided below. Use this list as a point of reference in your future studies. For now, just read the examples to get a sense of adverb use in English:

after (at a later or subsequent time)	*She's coming after three.*
again (once more)	*He did it again.*
almost (slightly short of, not quite)	*They're almost finished.*
already (before, by a specified time)	*He was already asleep when you called.*
also (in addition, besides)	*I will also stay, if you do.*
as a matter of fact (in fact, actually)	*As a matter of fact, he's already here.*
bad(ly) (awful, a lot)	*We wanted to be there bad(ly).*
barely (hardly, scarcely)	*We could barely see the road.*
by chance (accidentally, unintentionally)	*We ran into each other by chance.*
by now (already)	*By now we have come to expect this.*
early (near the start)	*It is too early to get up.*
enough (sufficient, adequate)	*He has had enough.*
far (distant)	*They live rather far.*
in a hurry (rushed)	*Why are you always in a hurry? Relax!*
in a little while (shortly)	*They are coming in a little while.*
in the meantime (temporarily)	*In the meantime we can watch TV.*
instead (in its place)	*He will go instead of me.*
just (now)	*They have just arrived.*
late (not on time)	*She is always late for her appointments.*

near(by) (close to)	*Doesn't he live near(by)?*
now (at present)	*What time is it now?*
nowadays (these days, today)	*Nowadays, life is far too stressful.*
only (merely)	*He did it only to impress you.*
rather (quite)	*She is rather pretty, don't you think?*
right away (immediately)	*I'll get to it right away.*
still (even now)	*He still loves her.*
then (after that, next)	*Come at noon. I'll be ready then.*
there (in that place)	*He lives there.*
too (also, as well)	*He too likes baseball.*
very (to a high degree, extremely)	*They are very happy*
yet (so far, until now)	*You have yet to say hello.*

9. In compound tenses and many phrasal constructions, adverbs can be put between the parts of verbal constructions (see Chapter 8):

They went out already.	or	*They already went out.*
We haven't finished working yet.	or	*We haven't yet finished working.*
This has been clearly demonstrated.	or	*This has been demonstrated clearly.*

10. Some must be put between:

She has just phoned.	not	*She has phoned just.*
She has never played that piece.	not	*She has played that piece never.*
We are simply amazed at their skills.	not	*We are amazed at their skills simply.*

11. Negative adverbs are discussed in Chapter 7.

Exercise Set 4-3

A. Change each word into an adverb of manner.

Example: slow
slowly

1. elegant
2. near
3. sincere
4. love
5. late
6. palpable
7. lucky
8. greedy
9. initial
10. wonderful

B. Fill in each blank with an appropriate adverb from pages 68–69.

1. They're coming _____ five o'clock.
2. Did you do that _____ , even though I told you not to?
3. They should make it on time, because they are _____ finished working.
4. He was _____ up by 5 A.M.
5. I will _____ try to come, if I have time.
6. There was so much fog that we could _____ see the road.
7. I ran into her yesterday _____ .
8. _____ you should know what to expect.
9. It is too early to get up. I went to bed very _____ last night.
10. She will go _____ of him.
11. What time is it _____ ?
12. We did it _____ to impress them.
13. I'll try to get to it _____ .
14. Come at four. I'll be ready _____ .
15. I like baseball; and my grandson _____ likes it.

Comparison

1. Adjectives and adverbs can be used to indicate that something or someone has a relatively equal, greater, or lesser degree of some quality or feature. Adjectives and adverbs by themselves are said to be in the *positive* degree. Use *as ... as* to indicate that two things (people, animals, objects, and so on) have the same or equal degree of some attribute, feature, and so on:

   Paula is as happy as her sister.
   This year's professors are as boring as last year's.
   She came to the party as willingly as you did.

2. The *comparative of majority* form of an adjective or adverb is used to indicate that one of two things (people, animals, objects, and so on) has more of some attribute, feature, and so on. An adjective or adverb is changed to this form either by adding the suffix *-er* to it or by using the quantifier *more* before it:

-er comparatives			*more* comparatives		
small	→	*smaller*	*wonderful*	→	*more wonderful*
sweet	→	*sweeter*	*beautiful*	→	*more beautiful*
late	→	*later*	*handsome*	→	*more handsome*

3. Note that if the adjective or adverb ends in a single vowel followed by *-d* or *-g*, the consonant is doubled when *-er* is added:

red	→	*redder*
big	→	*bigger*

4. Generally, if the adjective or adverb consists of one syllable, add *-er*; if it consists of more than one syllable, use *more*. This is just a rule of thumb:

One syllable			More than one syllable		
sweet	→	*sweeter*	*handsome*	→	*more handsome*
tough	→	*tougher*	*difficult*	→	*more difficult*
fast	→	*faster*	*quickly*	→	*more quickly*
slow	→	*slower*	*often*	→	*more often*

Exception: adjectives and adverbs ending in -y

happy	→	*happier*
trendy	→	*trendier*
messy	→	*messier*
lousy	→	*lousier*

5. Some adjectives and adverbs have irregular comparative forms:

bad(ly)	→	*worse*
far	→	*farther*
good	→	*better*
little	→	*less*
much	→	*more*
well	→	*better*

6. The *comparative of minority* form of an adjective or adverb is used to indicate that one of two things (people, animals, objects, and so on) has less of some attribute, feature, and so on. The degree of minority is formed with *less* before the adjective or adverb:

tall	→	*less tall*
small	→	*less small*
attractive	→	*less attractive*
generous	→	*less generous*

7. To compare different people, things, or situations with the same adjective or adverb, use *than* as shown:

She is a better athlete <u>than</u> I.
Mary is more studious <u>than</u> her sister.
Sarah is shorter <u>than</u> her brother.
Those boys are more generous <u>than</u> the others.
Those girls are less rambunctious <u>than</u> the other girls.

8. A sentence such as *She is a better athlete than I* is really an "elliptical version" (abbreviated version) of the sentence *She is a better athlete than I am.* That is why the subject form of the pronoun is used—*I* rather than *me: She is a better athlete than me.* However, the latter form is acceptable today in colloquial speech.

9. The *superlative* degree allows you to compare more than two things or people. To form the superlative, add *-est* to adjectives and adverbs that use *-er* in the comparative; otherwise replace *more* with *most* and *less* with *least*:

	Comparative	Superlative
	-er	*-est*
small	*smaller*	*(the) smallest*
tall	*taller*	*(the) tallest*
lovely	*lovelier*	*(the) loveliest*
simple	*simpler*	*(the) simplest*
	more	*most*
generous	*more generous*	*(the) most generous*
active	*more active*	*(the) most active*
usual	*more usual*	*(the) most usual*
sincere	*more sincere*	*(the) most sincere*
	less	*least*
generous	*less generous*	*(the) least generous*
tall	*less tall*	*(the) least tall*
simple	*less simple*	*(the) least simple*
sincere	*less sincere*	*(the) least sincere*

10. Note the following irregular forms:

	Comparative	**Superlative**
bad (ly)	*worse*	*(the) worst*
far	*farther*	*(the) farthest*
good	*better*	*(the) best*
little	*less*	*(the) least*
much	*more*	*(the) most*
well	*better*	*(the) best*

11. When superlatives are used in sentences, they must be preceded by the definite article:

Mary is the most studious person in her class.
He is the nicest person I have ever met.
Potatoes are the least expensive food items you can buy these days.
Mary is the most studious girl I know.

12. Note the use of the preposition *in* when the "comparison group" is indicated:

Mary is the most studious girl in that class.
He is the least courteous boy in the school.

Exercise Set 4-4

A. Complete the chart by providing the missing forms (if applicable).

Positive	Comparative of majority	Comparative of minority	Superlative of majority	Superlative of minority
tough				
	more useful			
		less tall		
				(the) least timid
bad				
	farther			
			(the) best	
good				
	less			

B. Fill in the blanks with the missing words.

1. Alex is the smartest person _____ the world.
2. I love the English language _____ much _____ you do, if not more.
3. Sarah is _____ most intelligent person I know.
4. Pluto is big; Neptune is bigger; Jupiter is the _____ .
5. Calculus is difficult; probability theory is less difficult; geometry is the _____ difficult.
6. You are the _____ friend I have ever had. You are absolutely great!

5

Pronouns

*As far as I'm concerned, "whom" is a word that was
invented to make everyone sound like a butler.*

Calvin Trillin (b. 1935)

Demonstrative and Possessive Pronouns

1. *Pronouns* are words used in place of nouns, substantives (words tak-
    ing on the function of nouns), or noun phrases (nouns accompanied
    by articles, demonstratives, adjectives, and so on). The noun that a
    pronoun replaces is called an *antecedent*:

Antecedent	Pronoun
<u>John</u> is American.	<u>He</u> is American.
<u>That book</u> belongs to Mary.	<u>That</u> belongs to Mary.
<u>That woman</u> is American.	<u>She</u> is American.
Give that book to <u>John</u>.	Give that book to <u>him</u>.
That is <u>my book</u>, not <u>your book</u>.	That book is <u>mine</u>, not <u>yours</u>.

2. This chapter will discuss all kinds of pronouns except interrogative
    pronouns. The latter will be taken up in Chapter 7.

3. *Demonstrative pronouns* replace antecedent noun phrases containing
    a demonstrative (Chapter 3). Notice that they have the same form
    of the demonstrative that begins the noun phrase:

Noun phrase	Demonstrative pronoun
<u>This drink</u> is delicious.	<u>This</u> is delicious
<u>These shoes</u> are small.	<u>These</u> are small.
<u>That novel</u> is new.	<u>That</u> is new.
<u>Those ideas</u> are well known.	<u>Those</u> are well known.

4. *Possessive pronouns* replace antecedent noun phrases containing a possessive adjective. As indicated in Chapter 3, the possessive pronouns are *mine, yours, his, hers, its, ours,* and *theirs.* They correspond to the possessive adjectives as shown:

Noun phrase	**Possessive pronoun**
<u>My</u> <u>fiancé</u> *is handsome.*	<u>Mine</u> *is handsome.*
<u>Your</u> <u>friend</u> *lives here.*	<u>Yours</u> *lives here.*
This is <u>his</u> <u>idea</u>.	*This is* <u>his</u>.
It is not <u>her</u> <u>idea</u>.	*It is not* <u>hers</u>.
<u>Our</u> <u>friends</u> *never go out.*	<u>Ours</u> *never go out.*
<u>Their</u> <u>friends</u> *always go out.*	<u>Theirs</u> *always go out.*

Exercise Set 5-1

A. Replace each italicized noun phrase with an appropriate demonstrative pronoun.

1. *That house* belongs to my daughter.
2. *Those cars* are brand new.
3. *This computer disk* has lots of memory.
4. *These forms* are too long to fill out.
5. Why did you buy *that magazine?*
6. What is *this device?*

B. Now, replace each italicized noun phrase with an appropriate possessive pronoun.

1. *My watch* is new.
2. *Their parents* are going abroad this year.
3. *Her friend* speaks English very well.
4. *His idea* is a good one.
5. *Your car* needs some repair.
6. *Our backyard* is full of weeds.

Personal Pronouns

1. *Personal pronouns* (*I, me, we, us,* and so on) are classified according to the person(s) speaking (first person), the person(s) spoken to (second person), or the person(s) spoken about (third person). The pronoun can, of course, be in the singular (referring to one person) or in the plural (referring to more than one person). Personal pronouns can function as subjects or objects of verbs:

   I am American.
   We too are American.
   Give that book to him, not to her.
   I really don't understand you.

2. *Subject pronouns,* as their name implies, function as the subjects of verbs (in both dependent and independent clauses).

   I love studying French.
   You are getting married, aren't you?
   They live nearby.

3. The subject pronouns are:

	Singular	Plural
first person	*I*	*we*
second person	*you*	*you*
third person (masculine)	*he*	*they*
third person (feminine)	*she*	*they*
third person (neuter)	*it*	*they*

4. Notice that *I* is capitalized no matter where it occurs in a sentence:

   In fact, I do not know how to speak German.
   Even if I do that, nothing will come of it.

5. In the third person, use *he or she* (or *she or he*) if the gender of the subject is not specified.

   Specified gender

   He is my brother.
   She is my sister.

Unspecified gender

Where is the person who was just here?
He or she left an umbrella on my desk.

The individual who said that is incorrect.
She or he should check it out.

6. When a collective noun (a noun that refers to a collection of people or things) refers to a single unit, use *it* instead:

   My family is fairly small. It consists of four people.

7. If the phrase refers instead to the actual individuals in the collectivity, use *they*:

   My family is always helpful. They are always willing to listen to me.

8. The pronoun *it* is classified as "neuter" because it can refer to an animate being whose gender is unspecified, an object, or an abstraction.

   Where is the book? It is on the table.
   Who is at the door? It is someone I do not recognize.
   Whose idea is that? It is my friend's idea.

9. *It* is also used

as the subject of an impersonal verb:

It is snowing.
It seems impossible.
It appears to be correct.
It costs a lot of money.

as an anticipatory sign:

Is it certain that they will win?
When is it going to happen, today or tomorrow?

Expletives

In sentences such as *It is true* and *There are too many people in this city*, *it* and *there* are called *expletives*.

Expletives have no meaning in a vocabulary sense.

There introduces the idea that something exists in a particular place:

There is a book on the table.
There are seven books on the table.

It is sometimes called a "dummy subject" because it fills a subject slot that would otherwise be empty:

It is exactly what I mean.
It is not necessary to say that.

---

to refer to a general condition or state of affairs:

She couldn't stand it.
It was necessary.

informally, to refer to something that is the best, the most desir-
able, or without equal:

He thinks he's it!
That steak was really it!

10. As their name implies, *object pronouns* function as objects of verbs.
As discussed in Chapter 1, an object can be direct or indirect. Look
up the definitions of these terms if you have forgotten them:

Direct object	Indirect object
Mary calls <u>her</u> every evening.	*Mary is speaking to <u>her</u> right now.*
She does not believe <u>me</u>.	*Give it to <u>me</u>.*

11. The direct and indirect object pronouns are listed below. The indirect ones are often preceded by *to* or *for*:

	Singular		**Plural**	
	Direct	**Indirect**	**Direct**	**Indirect**
first person	*me*	*(to / for) me*	*us*	*(to / for) us*
second person	*you*	*(to / for) you*	*you*	*(to / for) you*
third person (masculine)	*him*	*(to / for) him*	*them*	*(to / for) them*
third person (feminine)	*her*	*(to / for) her*	*them*	*(to / for) them*
third person (neuter)	*it*	*(to / for) it*	*them*	*(to / for) them*

Mary calls <u>me</u> every day.
I'll call <u>you</u> in a half-hour.
Mary calls <u>him</u> every day.
Mary e-mails <u>her</u> often.

Sir, I'll call <u>you</u> tomorrow.
Why don't you call <u>us</u>?
I'll call <u>them</u> after.

Mary speaks to <u>me</u> every week.
I'll speak to <u>you</u> about it in a month.
Mary speaks to <u>him</u> often.
But she does not speak to <u>her</u> very often.

Sir, may I speak to <u>you</u>?
Why don't you speak to <u>us</u> anymore?
I don't speak to <u>them</u> anymore.

12. If you use the indirect object pronoun before a direct object, you must drop the preposition:

John gave the book to _me_.   John gave _me_ the book
He gave the medicine to _them_.   He gave _them_ the medicine.

13. The object pronouns are also used after prepositions:

She never comes _with_ _me_ to the movies.
He spoke _about_ _us_ throughout his lecture.

Exercise Set 5-2

A. In each sentence there is an incorrect personal pronoun form. Provide the correct one.

1. John and i are going out together.
2. Who is that man? It is my brother.
3. My sister always calls when he or she has free time.
4. We are our parents.
5. Where is my watch? There is on the desk.
6. Mary calls I every evening.
7. Do it for we!
8. I spoke to he yesterday.
9. That belongs to she.
10. Who are them?
11. Speak to they.

B. Choose the appropriate answer, (a) or (b).

1. Who wrote that? _____ is someone I do not recognize.
   (a) It
   (b) She

2. _____ looks like a fun thing to do.
   (a) It
   (b) There

3. How many books are ____ on that shelf?
   (a) it
   (b) there

4. When is ____ finally going to happen?
   (a) it
   (b) there

5. She thinks she's ____ .
   (a) it
   (b) there

6. Mary and ____ love to go to the movies.
   (a) me
   (b) I

Reflexive and Reciprocal Pronouns

1. *Reflexive* pronouns are words that "reflect" the subject of a verb; that is, they refer to the same person or thing as the subject of the sentence. Like object pronouns, they generally come after the verb:

   <u>My sister</u> washes <u>herself</u> *every night before going to sleep.*
   <u>They</u> *always enjoy* <u>themselves</u> *on vacation.*

2. The reflexive pronouns are as follows. Notice that they end in *-self* in the singular and *-selves* in the plural:

	Singular	**Plural**
first person	*myself*	*ourselves*
second person	*yourself*	*yourselves*
third person (masculine)	*himself*	*themselves*
third person (feminine)	*herself*	*themselves*
third person (neuter)	*itself*	*themselves*
third person (generic)	*oneself*	*themselves*

I always enjoy <u>myself</u> at the movies.
Please introduce <u>yourself</u>.
<u>They</u> have already introduced <u>themselves</u>.
<u>We</u> will do it <u>ourselves</u>.
<u>He</u> considers <u>himself</u> to be rather intelligent.
<u>She</u> also considers <u>herself</u> to be quite intelligent.
Don't worry. <u>The situation</u> will take care of <u>itself</u>.
<u>One</u> always enjoys <u>oneself</u> at those family events.

3. Reflexive pronouns are also used for emphasis:

   I did it myself!
   She wrote the report herself, with no help!

4. The expression *by* + *reflexive pronoun* conveys the idea of being alone:

She lives by herself.	or	She lives alone.
I live by myself.	or	I live alone.

5. *Each other* and *one another* are called *reciprocal pronouns*. The former is preferred when referring to two nouns, and the latter when referring to more than two nouns:

   John and Mary love each other.
   The members of that club respect one another.

Exercise Set 5-3

A. Fill in the blanks with the appropriate reflexive or reciprocal pronouns.

   1. My cousin and his fiancée really adore _____ .
   2. He always does those things _____ !
   3. The workers in that company support _____ .
   4. Do you live by _____ ?
   5. One should always look after _____ .
   6. The situation will work _____ out.
   7. She considers _____ to be beautiful.
   8. We tried to do it _____ , but couldn't.
   9. They worry only about _____ .
   10. I'm not sure I can do it by _____ .

B. Here is a quick grammar review for you. Complete the chart by filling in the missing pronouns:

Subject	Direct object	Indirect object	Possessive	Reflexive
I	them	(to) us		
				yourself
he				yourselves
	her			
			its	

Relative Pronouns

1. As discussed in Chapter 1, complex sentences are made up of a main clause (called the independent clause) and one or more dependent clauses. A *relative clause*, such as an adjective clause, for example, is introduced by a *relative pronoun*. The relative pronouns are

who
introduces a clause when the antecedent is a person or persons:

The person who is reading the newspaper is my sister.
Those are the people who are coming to the party.

that
introduces a clause whose antecedent is not a person:

The dress that I bought yesterday is very beautiful.
I love the poem that you are reading.

In informal speech it is also used to refer to people

The man that (instead of who) you saw yesterday is my brother.

which
introduces a clause that provides additional information about the antecedent or defines the antecedent in some way:

My house, <u>which</u> is small and old, is still home to me.
The movie <u>which</u> was shown later was better.

that which / what
introduces a clause that restricts the antecedent in some way:

He bought <u>that which</u> he needed. / He bought <u>what</u> he needed.

what
is used when the antecedent follows, particularly in formal style:

Still, he has not said he will withdraw, <u>which</u> is more surprising.

but

Still, <u>what</u> (not which) is more surprising, he has not said he will withdraw.

those who
is used to refer to a generic subject:

Those who say that do not know what they are talking about.

2. After prepositions, *who* is replaced by *whom*. Both *that* and *which* are replaced by *which* after prepositions:

   <u>To whom</u> did you give the letter?
   The drawer <u>in which</u> I put the watch is over there.

3. Although falling out of use because of its level of formality, *whom* is also used to introduce clauses that have an object function:

   He is the man <u>whom</u> I met last night.

4. The possessive form of these pronouns is *whose*:

   He is a man <u>whose</u> power has been greatly reduced.
   The play, <u>whose</u> style is very formal, is typical of the period.

5. Pronouns ending in -ever replace general antecedents; for example, *whoever* replaces a person antecedent, and *whichever / whatever* all other kinds of antecedents:

    <u>*Whoever*</u> *goes to Florida will enjoy himself or herself.*
    It's a long trip <u>*whichever / whatever*</u> *road you take.*

6. Here is a list:

    whoever/whomever   **anyone who(m)**

    <u>*Whoever*</u> *wants to come to the party is welcome.*
    I make friends with <u>*whomever*</u> *I meet.*

    whatever   **anything that**

    I always say <u>*whatever*</u> *comes to my mind.*

    whichever   **anyone that**

    We can go to <u>*whichever*</u> *movie you prefer.*

    whenever   **any time that**

    We can go to the movies <u>*whenever*</u> *you want.*

    wherever   **anywhere that**

    We can go <u>*wherever*</u> *you want on holidays.*

    however   **in any way that**

    You may dress <u>*however*</u> *you want to go to the movies with us.*

Exercise Set 5-4

A. Fill in the blanks with the missing relative pronouns.

1. The woman _____ is reading the newspaper is my sister.
2. They are the people _____ are coming to our party.
3. My car, _____ is brand new, is always giving me problems.
4. The book _____ I read yesterday was better than the one I read two weeks ago.

5. The jacket _____ I bought yesterday is much too tight.
6. I love the piano piece _____ you are performing tonight.
7. Those _____ believe him will soon find out that they have been duped.
8. She bought only _____ she needed.
9. _____ is really shocking is that they didn't even mention a word about the incident.
10. To _____ did you speak yesterday?
11. The shelf on _____ I put the book is rather high.
12. She is the woman _____ I met last night.
13. That is a nation _____ influence over international affairs has been greatly reduced.
14. The song, _____ style is very jazzy, is typical of that genre.

B. Choose the appropriate answer, (a) or (b).

1. _____ wants to play along is quite welcome.
   (a) Whoever
   (b) Whomever

2. She always says _____ comes to her mind.
   (a) whichever
   (b) whatever

3. We can go to _____ game you prefer.
   (a) whenever
   (b) whichever

4. We can go to the baseball game _____ you want.
   (a) whenever
   (b) wherever

5. We can go _____ you want tonight; it makes no difference to me where we go.
   (a) whenever
   (b) wherever

6. You may dress _____ you want for your wedding.
   (a) however
   (b) wherever

Indefinite and Impersonal Pronouns

1. *Indefinite pronouns*, such as *any* and *some*, replace quantity antecedents (Chapter 3). *Impersonal pronouns*, such as *one* and *somebody*, refer to people in a general or nonspecific way:

   I ate only <u>some</u>.
   <u>Somebody</u> said that yesterday, but I don't know who.

2. When referring to people or things in general, use the pronouns *many, some, someone, anybody, everything, a lot, few, several, all, everyone, anyone,* and so on.

   <u>Many</u> are going to France this year.
   <u>Some</u> sleep in the morning, but quite <u>a few</u> go to work early.
   <u>Everyone</u> knows that.
   <u>Somebody</u> called for you last night.
   <u>Anybody</u> who wants to come is welcome.

3. Note that some are singular and thus require a singular verb:

   anyone
   anything
   each
   either
   everybody
   everything
   neither
   no one
   nobody
   one
   other
   someone
   something

4. A few indefinite pronouns end in *-ever*:

   <u>Whichever</u> you give me is fine with me.
   <u>Wherever</u> you go, I will follow you.
   <u>Whenever</u> you come, you are welcome.
   <u>However</u> you do it, you must do it in good faith.

5. Notice the indefinite expression *some ... others*:

   Some will go to Italy; others, instead, will go to France.

6. The indefinite pronoun *there* is an expletive used to introduce a clause or sentence referring to unspecified things:

   There are numerous items on the agenda.
   There must be another exit.

7. The pronoun *there* is also used to indicate an unspecified person in direct address:

   Hello there.

8. To refer to an indefinitely specified individual, use *one*, which means "any person in general":

> **Differences in Usage**
>
> Different pronouns may be used in the same sentence to refer back to one:
>
> *One should look after one's health.*
> *One should look after his or her health.*
>
> The first one is typical of formal usage, while the second is being used more and more today.

   The older one grows, the more one is supposed to understand things.

9. *You* can also be used instead, although it is much less formal than *one*:

   The older you grow, the more you are supposed to understand things.

10. The personal pronoun *they* can also be used as an impersonal pronoun to mean "people," "some people," or "somebody":

    They say that the climate   or   *Some people say that the*
       is changing.   *climate is changing.*

11. The pronoun *other*, in its various forms (*other, another, others, the other*), is used as either an adjective or a pronoun. The meaning of *another* is "one more in addition to the one(s) already indicated," whereas *other(s)* means "several more in addition to the one(s) indicated," and *the other(s)* means "what is left over from a given number":

    One of the students is from the United States; another is from Canada.
    Other students are from South America.
    Others still are from Europe.
    That student is from Mexico; the other student is from Peru.

12. Finally, notice the meanings of the following useful pronouns:

    one another / each other
    for expressing mutual action or relationship:

    We call <u>one another / each other</u> almost every day.
    They phone <u>each other</u> every night.
    We write to <u>one another</u> every month.

    every other
    for expressing alternation:

    We call each other <u>every other</u> day.

    one after the other, one after another
    for expressing sequence:

    The students started filing out of the room <u>one after the other</u>.
    They filed out <u>one after another</u>.

    in other words
    to clarify the preceding clause(s):

    <u>In other</u> words, you should do what I say.

    the other day (a few days ago)
    as a time expression:

    I ran into her just <u>the other day</u>.

    other than
    except:

    No one understands me <u>other than</u> my best friend.

Exercise Set 5-5

A. There is an error in each sentence. Find it and correct it.

1. They drink quite a lots.
2. No one speak Spanish here.
3. Everyone are going to Italy this year.
4. Some work in the evening, but much work in the daytime.
5. Many knows that.
6. Anybodies who wants to come is welcome.
7. Anything are better than nothing.
8. Somethings is bothering her.
9. Whichever you go, I will follow you.
10. Some will study in the United States; other, instead, will study in their own countries.
11. There is many things to do.
12. Hello you. How are you?

B. Choose the appropriate answer, (a) or (b).

1. The older one becomes, the more _____ is supposed to slow down at work.
   (a) one
   (b) you

2. The richer you become, the more _____ are expected to be generous.
   (a) one
   (b) you

3. Whatever _____ say, it is simply not true!
   (a) they
   (b) anyone

4. One of the students is from Brazil; _____ are from here.
   (a) one
   (b) the others

5. They call _____ almost daily.
   (a) one another
   (b) every other

6. They call each other _____ day.
   (a) one another
   (b) every other

7. They started leaving _____ .
   (a) one after the other
   (b) other than

6

Prepositions, Conjunctions, and Interjections

Expression shall be vital and natural, as much as the voice of a brute or an interjection.

Henry David Thoreau (1817–1862)

What Are Prepositions?

1. A *preposition* (literally, "something positioned before") is a word that comes before some other part of speech, generally a noun, substantive, or noun phrase, to show its relationship to some other part in the sentence. You can recognize prepositions easily—they are short words such as *in* and *by* that indicate location, direction, position, time, and many other such useful notions.

    He was <u>in</u> the car.
    She will be here <u>by</u> ten o'clock.

2. Prepositions have many, many uses. All of them cannot be mentioned in a basic handbook. Below you will find a comprehensive list of prepositions as used in common phrases. Use it as a reference guide or "mini-dictionary." Look up each preposition in a dictionary and then read the examples below so that you can get a good sense of how the prepositions are used in English. There really is no other way to learn how to use prepositions!

    about

    There are about twenty miles to go.
    Did you read that book about insects?
    The band is about to play.

above

You can see it above the roof.
I could not hear you above the music.
It has been somewhat above normal temperature the entire month.
The water was above my shoulders.

across

They live across the street.
Draw these lines across the paper.
The town is across the river.
Yesterday I came across my old schoolmate.

after

The letter B comes after A.
You must go after the big money.
She looked after her mother for years.
Come after dinner!
They are still friends after all their differences.
They go there year after year.
He was named after a great hero.
He's a person after my own heart.
It's five minutes after three.

against

We had to swim against the current.
Do not lean against the wall; we just painted it.
I did it against my better judgment.
I bought that jacket as protection against the cold.

along

There were many trees along the avenue.
The members split over the issue along political lines.

among

They are among the wealthy.
That is a custom popular among Mexicans.
Don't fight among yourselves!

around

There are hundreds of trees around that park.
You have to wear this around your waist.
They live just around the corner.
I usually get up around seven.
Their economy revolves around tourism.

at

I'll meet you at the mall.
They came at us from all sides.
Let's meet at six o'clock.
He's really good at math.
You can buy that at five dollars a pound.
They rejoiced at their team's victory.
He exited at the rear gate.

before

They came before ten o'clock.
His whole life lies before him.
The case is now before the courts.
The prince is before his brother in the line of succession.

behind

He sat behind her.
The broom is behind the door.
Their worries are behind them.
The plane was behind schedule.
Behind your every action is self-interest.

below

They live below us.
It is twenty degrees below zero.

beneath

The earth lay beneath a blanket of snow.
It is beneath me to beg.

beside

She has earned a place beside the best performers in classical music.
Their office is beside the elevator.
That remark was beside the point.

between

I saw him between the trees.
It costs between 100 and 200 dollars.
There are a lot of common things between the two stories.
Between them they succeeded.
You must choose between medicine and music as a career.

beyond

He threw it just beyond the fence.
I studied well beyond midnight.
He became rich beyond his wildest dreams.
She asked for nothing beyond peace and quiet.

by

Put that flower pot on the table by the door.
We came by the back road.
We drove by your house.
She sleeps by day and works by night.
Please be there by 5:30 P.M.
He buys CDs by the hundreds every year.
They never play by the rules.
They are siblings by blood.

Your grandfather was killed by a bullet.
Multiply 4 by 6 to get 24.
That room is twelve by eighteen feet.
They went north by northwest.
They traveled by train.
Hamlet was written by Shakespeare.

despite

They won the game despite overwhelming odds.

down

He threw it down the hill
I saw the raft floating down the river.
Keep walking down the street and you will find my house at the end.

during

They arrived during the storm.
During the war many atrocities took place.

for

She has plans to run for senator.
They headed off for town.
He is eager for fame and fortune.
They prepared lunch for us.
He spoke for all the members.
Were they for or against the proposal?
Is that a substitute for eggs?
We paid 200 dollars for a ticket.
I took two steps back for every step forward.
We walked and walked for miles.
I had an appointment for two o'clock.
You cannot take that for granted.
For one thing, we can't afford it.
We jumped for joy.
He is a stickler for neatness.
She was named for her grandmother.

from

I'm free from six o'clock on.
I had her from grade four to grade six.
I got that book from the shelf.
It's hard to keep them from making a mistake.
They do not know right from wrong.
She was feeling faint from hunger.

in

They were born in the fall.
He threw the paper in the wastebasket.
They are no longer in debt.
He has spent his life in politics.
They arranged to purchase the car in equal payments.
That poem is written in understandable language.
He is a tall man in an overcoat.
We paid for it in cash.
That note is written in German.
They followed in pursuit.
I have faith in your judgment.
Only one in ten usually wins.
You're in for a big surprise.

like

It's not like him to take offense.
They have always lived like royalty.
He felt like studying math.
It looks like a good year for farmers.
They saved things like old newspapers.

near

He is staying at an inn near London.
They live near the mall.
The movie is almost near the end.

of

They are citizens of the north.
They live a mile east of here.
We were robbed of our dignity.
He always gives of his time.
She wore a dress of silk.
He is a man of ideas.
Those are the rungs of a ladder.
She is a person of honor.
That was very nice of you.
He had a basket of groceries when he arrived.
What is the Leaning Tower of Pisa?
She has always had a love of horses.
Those are all products of the vine.
They just experienced a year of famine.
I think highly of her proposals.

off

The insect fell off the branch.
Today I am off duty.
He has been living off meat and potatoes.
She has been off her game.
My house is just off the interstate.

on

The vase is on the table.
The cat jumped on the table.
Independence Day is on July fourth.
On entering the room, she saw him.
The spotlight fell on the actress.
He cut his foot on the broken glass.
We went on a strict diet.
We will reach our goal on deeds and on results.
He's on the way.
He is away on business.
She's a nurse on the hospital staff.
That's a book on astrology.

I haven't a cent on me.
The drinks are on the house.
They swore on the Bible to tell the truth.

out

Our cat fell out the window.
Out this door is the driveway.

over

There's a new sign over the door.
To get there you must jump over the fence and then go over the bridge.
They live in a village over the border.
Put a coat of varnish over the woodwork.
I have already looked over the report.
She threw a shawl over her shoulders.
They won a narrow victory over their longtime rivals.
There is no one over him in the department.
What change has come over you?
Let's have a chat over coffee.
Their argument was over methods.

through

We went through the tunnel.
They went for a walk through the flowers.
They climbed in through the window.
They bought the antique vase through a dealer.
We took a tour through France.
They stayed up through the night.
We are through the initial testing period.
That play will run through December.
I drove through a red light without thinking.
She succeeded through hard work.
That suit is wet through and through.

throughout

The tunnel is open throughout the year.

till / until

They danced till / until dawn.
She can't leave till / until Sunday.

to

He went to the city.
The ocean water was clear all the way to the bottom.
That law is meant to help minority women achieve economic equality.
They looked outside with their faces pressed to the window.
They stood face to face.
I am waiting for an answer to my e-mail.
The brook runs parallel to the road.
We all danced to the tune.
Are there two cups to a pint?
Those responsibilities are suited to her abilities.
His latest book is superior to his others.
The time is ten to five.
He went out to lunch.
Refer to a dictionary.

under

Put that rug under your chair.
The gas pipes are under the ground.
She traveled under a false name.
There are nine officers under me at headquarters.
They no longer live under a dictatorship.
He is under constant care.
You are under contract.
That law is under discussion.
She was born under the sign of Aries.

up

You have to climb up the hill first.
We live just two miles up the road.

with

Did you go with her?
He sat with his family.
She arrived with good news.
He performed that piece with skill.
They left the dog with the neighbors.
If it's all right with you, I'll go ahead and buy it.
We planted onions with the carrots.
They play with a symphony orchestra.
You have to eat that with a fork.
Even with all her experience, she could not get that job.
He gets up with the birds.
We are pleased with her decision.
That dress is identical with the one her sister just bought.
He loves to wrestle with that opponent.
We are sick with the flu.
Wines improve with age.

within

He has strong emotions within him.
You should arrive within two days.
We live within ten miles of your house.
You must always act within the law.
The team had pulled to within five points of winning.

without

She volunteered without hesitation.
He spoke without thinking.

3. Some prepositions are made up of more than one word used with other parts of speech: *adhere to, envious of, expert in, foreign to, in addition to, as well as, identical to, different from, prior to, profit by, sensitive to,* and *tamper with.* These are just a few of the idiomatic prepositional phrases that you will simply have to memorize as you come across them in your studies.

Exercise Set 6-1

A. Fill in the blanks with the missing prepositions.

1. There are _____ fifty miles to go before we reach Chicago.
2. The temperature has been _____ normal the entire winter.
3. The store is just _____ the street.
4. Let's go to the movies _____ dinner, not before.
5. It's just a few minutes _____ five.
6. Do not lean _____ the fence; we just painted it.
7. The sidewalk runs all _____ the avenue.
8. He is now _____ the very wealthy.
9. Our house is just _____ the corner.
10. I usually go to bed _____ ten.
11. I'll meet you _____ the movies.
12. I'll see you _____ seven o'clock.
13. She's really good _____ piano-playing.
14. They came _____ ten o'clock.
15. He sat _____ her throughout school.
16. Everyone is _____ schedule, unfortunately.
17. Such behavior is _____ you.
18. It is _____ me to beg.
19. He has earned a place _____ the best thinkers in America.
20. You must choose _____ him and her.
21. I prepared lunch _____ you.
22. We walked and walked _____ hours.
23. She was named _____ a Biblical character.
24. I'm free _____ five o'clock on.
25. Don't you know right _____ wrong any longer?
26. They're both born _____ September.
27. That man has spent his entire life _____ politics.
28. You can pay for it _____ cash.
29. You're in _____ a big surprise.
30. They have always lived _____ privileged people.
31. They are staying at a hotel _____ Chicago.
32. We live _____ the mall.
33. Our home is a few miles _____ here.
34. That was very nice _____ her.
35. I think highly _____ her musicianship.

B. Now match the parts in the two columns logically to make complete sentences.

1. I did it _____ .
2. They should be arriving _____ .
3. He always comes _____ .
4. For now, everything is _____ .
5. The outcome is still _____ .
6. Both studied for the exam right _____ .
7. He studies constantly _____ .
8. I cannot do it _____ at the very earliest.
9. Would you like to go _____ at noon?
10. The cat always sleeps _____ .
11. To lose a lot of weight, you must go _____ .
12. Why don't you stop by? We are _____ .
13. I threw the cat _____ !
14. There is a sign _____ .
15. I have been teaching for _____ .
16. I spilled some milk _____ .
17. I'm not working today; I'm _____ .
18. We decided to head _____ this afternoon.
19. He has decided to run _____ .
20. The lights went off _____ .
21. The logs were floating _____ .
22. We'll be driving _____ , so we'll drop in.
23. You have to play _____ !
24. Why don't you come _____ , instead of driving?
25. He achieved success _____ .
26. I cannot stay up _____ .

(a) beyond midnight
(b) by your house
(c) by the rules
(d) by bike
(e) despite overwhelming odds
(f) down the river
(g) during dinner
(h) for senator
(i) for the movies
(j) off duty
(k) on the floor
(l) on a strict diet
(m) on the way
(n) out the door
(o) over the door
(p) over fifty years
(q) through the night
(r) throughout the year
(s) until tomorrow
(t) to lunch
(u) under the sofa
(v) under discussion
(w) up in the air
(x) with good news
(y) within a few days
(z) without thinking

C.   Now choose the noun or noun phrase following the preposition that best suits the meaning, (a) or (b).

1. You must never be _____ others.
    (a) adhere to
    (b) envious of

2. He is an _____ probability theory.
    (a) expert in
    (b) foreign to

3. We should eat _____ the concert.
    (a) prior to
    (b) as well as

4. She is quite _____ her brother.
    (a) in addition to
    (b) different from

5. Ultimately, you will not _____ taking advantage of others.
    (a) identical to
    (b) profit by

6. A good lawyer will never _____ the evidence.
    (a) tamper with
    (b) sensitive to

Two Tricky Prepositions

1. Two prepositions are particularly tricky and are often confused in the uses indicated below. They thus require just a little more attention. The prepositions in question are *in* and *on*.

2. Use *in* to indicate

    driving, walking, strolling, and so on, in weather conditions:

    I do not like driving in the snow.
    Walking in the rain is not a good idea.

living, staying, remaining, and so on, in a place:

I live in New York.
I am staying in the United States as a visiting student.

being, staying, and so on, inside somewhere:

He's in the house.
She's getting in the car as we speak.

a general time frame:

I'll see you in the morning.
I always fall asleep in the afternoon.

a specific month:

I'll see you in January.
They're leaving in June.

3. Use *on* to indicate

a specific day:

I'll see you on Monday.
She's leaving on Saturday.

a recurrent date or event:

They go to church on Sundays.
We always go on vacation when we can.

boarding:

He just got on the boat.
I had difficulty getting on that horse.

Exercise Set 6-2

A.   Use *in* or *on* as the case may be.

1. Going out for a walk _____ the pouring rain is not a good idea.
2. Let's meet _____ Wednesday. OK?
3. We always go out _____ Saturdays.
4. We're going _____ vacation soon.
5. They live _____ San Francisco.
6. I am staying _____ the country as a tourist.
7. He's working _____ the garage.
8. She's getting _____ the van as we speak.
9. I'll see you _____ the afternoon.
10. We're going _____ June.
11. He just got _____ the plane.

B.   Replace each italicized phrase with another one starting with *in* or *on*, as the case may be.

1. He goes to the mall *every Saturday*.
2. They are leaving *this Friday*.
3. I'll call you *tomorrow morning*.
4. I do not like traveling *during thunderstorms*.
5. The game will be on *throughout the afternoon*.

What Are Conjunctions?

1. A *conjunction* is a word—such as *and*, *but*, *as*, or *because*—that connects words, phrases, clauses, or sentences. Conjunctions are "connectors" that show the relationship between words, phrases, and so on.

Alex <u>and</u> Sarah are brother <u>and</u> sister.
<u>Either</u> he <u>or</u> I will do that.
<u>As</u> part of your reward, you will get an extended holiday.
He likes to ski a lot <u>because</u> he is an athletic person.

2. Conjunctions, like prepositions, have many, many uses. Again, all of them cannot be mentioned in a basic handbook. Nevertheless, a comprehensive list of conjunctions is provided here for your convenience and future reference.

3. There are three main types of conjunctions: subordinating, coordinating, and correlative. *Subordinating conjunctions* are used to connect independent clauses and other subordinate structures to a main clause. Here are a few subordinating conjunctions:

after

I saw them after you arrived.

although / even though / though

Although I like opera, I will not sit through that one.
Even though she sings well, she prefers to be anything but a singer.
Though I like opera, I still fall asleep during most performances.

as

Think as I think.
He slipped on the ice as he ran home.
I went to bed early, as I was exhausted.
The sun is hot, as everyone knows.

because

She did it because she likes it.

before

See me before you leave.
I will die before I will betray my country.

if

If I were to go, I would be late.
If that is true, what should we do?
Ask if he plans to come to the meeting.
If only they had come earlier!

If you mix red and blue, you will get purple.
If I were you, I would look for another home.

though

Though they may not succeed, they will still try.

when

I like the spring when the snow melts.
I'll call you when I get there.
How can he get good grades when he won't study?
When I finally got to the airport, my plane had already taken off.

3. The conjunctions *and, but, or, so, for, yet,* and *nor* are used primarily to connect words or phrases that have the same function (two nouns, two verbs, and so on). They are called *coordinating conjunctions*. For a discussion of their meanings, see Chapter 1.

> **Commas**
>
> No commas are required if there are only two parts to be conjoined:
>
> *Bill and Mary love hot dogs (not Bill, and Mary love hot dogs).*
>
> Commas are used if more than two parts are conjoined:
>
> *Bill, Jill, and Mary love hot dogs.*
>
> Commas can be used when clauses are joined:
>
> *Alex is coming to the party, but Janis is staying at home.*

Alex <u>and</u> his friend are coming as well.
She wants to watch TV <u>or</u> read tonight.
The shoes are tight <u>but</u> comfortable.
Heather is sick, <u>so</u> she's not going out.
She is sick, <u>for</u> she went out in the cold.
She is not sick, <u>nor</u> is she tired.
She said she would be late, <u>yet</u> she arrived on time.

4. Some conjunctions are paired with other conjunctions or other parts of speech. These are called *paired* or *correlative conjunctions*:

both ... and

Both his sister and his mother adore him.

not only ... but also

He is adored not only by his sister but also by his mother.

either ... or / neither ... nor

She will major in either biology or psychology.
That movie is neither entertaining nor instructive.

but ... anyway / but ... still

It was cold, but I went swimming anyway.
It was cold, but I still went swimming.

Exercise Set 6-3

A. Use an appropriate subordinating or coordinating conjunction in each blank, as the case may be.

1. We decided to go out _____ we had finished dinner.
2. _____ I like music, I cannot listen to that particular song any longer.
3. _____ he finds math easy, he prefers to be anything but a mathematician.
4. I stumbled on the sidewalk _____ I ran home.
5. Our winters are cold, _____ everyone knows.
6. Alex loves math _____ he loves music.
7. Mark _____ Mary should do that, not you.
8. The pants are tight _____ comfortable.
9. I am not well, _____ I'm not coming.
10. I am not bored, _____ am I tired.
11. I always watch baseball _____ I like it.
12. Call me _____ you leave.
13. _____ that is the case, what should I do?
14. _____ she may not succeed, she will still try.
15. We'll call you _____ we get there.

B.   Missing from each sentence is one of the parts of a correlative conjunction. Supply it in each case.

1.   Both Jim _____ his friend play baseball.
2.   He is good _____ at music but also in sports.
3.   She will grow up to be either a doctor _____ a lawyer.
4.   That song is _____ melodious nor rhythmic.
5.   It was pouring rain, _____ I went swimming anyway.

What Are Interjections?

1.   An *interjection* is a word expressing some emotion or attitude that is capable of standing alone, for example, *Ugh!* or *Wow!*
2.   Here are some common interjections. Note that they are followed by either an exclamation point or a question mark:

Ah! (expresses satisfaction, surprise, delight, dislike, or pain)

Ah! Now do you know what I mean?
Ah! Why did you do that?

How come? (expresses disbelief)

You're late! How come?

Huh! (expresses surprise, contempt, or indifference)

Huh? What do you mean?

No matter! (in fact; actually)

No matter, you are correct!
No matter, I couldn't have done it!
I'm taking that bus, no matter where it's going!

Oh! (expresses surprise, fear, anger, pain)

Oh dear! I forgot my keys again.

Ouch! (expresses sudden pain or displeasure)

Ouch! I didn't realize that the stove was on.

So! (expresses surprise or comprehension)

So! You've finished your work at last!

Ugh! (expresses horror, disgust, or repugnance)

Ugh! That color makes me sick!

What? (expresses disbelief)

What? I don't believe it!

Wow! (expresses wonder, amazement, or great pleasure)

Wow! They finally won!

Exercise Set 6-4

A. Match the interjections in the left-hand column with the statements in the right-hand column.

1. Ah!		(a)	It can't be true!
2. What?		(b)	We finally beat them!
3. Ugh!		(c)	Why did you say that?
4. So!		(d)	That medicine makes me vomit!
5. Wow!		(e)	You're here at last!

B. What interjections could you use to express each of the following emotions?

1. anger
2. sudden pain
3. in fact
4. surprise
5. disbelief
6. delight

Other Joining Words

1. There are some words, such as *however* and *therefore*, that are difficult to locate in a simplified framework of grammar. Basically, these are words that allow you to express such things as contrast, transition, consequence, and so on. Generally, they function as conjunctions or as adverbs. Most often they are conjunctive adverbs used in compound sentences to connect independent clauses, and their placement can vary:

   However he did it, it was very clever.
   You are right; therefore, I am mistaken.
   I was tired; therefore, I went to bed early.
   I was tired; I didn't go to bed early, however.
   She is neat; her husband, however, is messy.

2. They can also connect ideas between separate sentences:

   I was tired. Therefore, I went to bed early.

3. Here is a brief list of common words of this type:

   however

   However he did it, it was very clever.
   However reluctantly, I must acknowledge your concerns.
   The book is expensive; however, it's worth it.
   The first part was easy; the second, however, took hours.
   Dress however you like.

   maybe

   Maybe he's right.
   Maybe I'll go too.

   nevertheless

   Even though you are right, you should nevertheless help out.

   no

   No, I'm not going.
   That's no better than what you gave me yesterday.

only

There is room for only one passenger.
If you would only come home.
Those are facts known only to us.
Those actions will only make things worse.
They called me only last month.
You may go, only be careful.
The merchandise is well made, only we can't use it.

therefore

As Descartes said, "I think, therefore I am!"
I worked through lunch, therefore I am now hungry.

thus

Lay the pieces out thus.
Thus it was necessary for me to resign.
Few play that well; thus they expect you to do so.

yes

Yes. I'll do it.
Yes? Did she really say that?
Yes! It's about time!

4. A word that is used (and abused) pervasively in common speech is
    like. Here's what you should know about it:

as a preposition:

She's just like her brother.
It's not like you to take offense.
They have always lived like royalty.
I felt like running away.
It looks like a bad year for farmers.
I have always saved things like old newspapers and magazines.

as an adjective:

On this and like occasions, I always dress up.

as an adverb:

He ran like crazy.

as a noun:

I ate carrots, potatoes, and the like.
I've never seen the likes of this before.

as a conjunction:

To dance like she does requires great discipline.
It looks like we'll finish on time.

Exercise Set 6-5

A.   Supply an appropriate "joining word" to complete each sentence.

   1. I always work through lunch, and, _____ , I am always hungry at the end of the day.
   2. Few know as much as you do; _____ they expect you to take the lead.
   3. _____ , I'll do it.
   4. _____ , she's not coming.
   5. There's room in the car for _____ one other person.
   6. The essay is difficult; _____ , it's worth reading.
   7. _____ I should go too.
   8. Although you are right, you should _____ keep quiet about it.

B.   Choose the appropriate answer, (a) or (b).

   1. To play like _____ involves great discipline.
      (a) she does
      (b) she'll finish

   2. He loves riddles, acrostics, crosswords, _____ .
      (a) and the like
      (b) and the likes

3. He had to do well on that exam, so he studied like _____ .
   (a) never before in his life
   (b) well

4. On this and _____ occasions, I always dress up.
   (a) like
   (b) likes

5. He's just _____ her.
   (a) likes
   (b) like

7

Interrogatives and Negatives

It is not every question that deserves an answer.

Publilius Syrus (First century BCE)

What Are Interrogatives?

1. Interrogatives are words that allow you to ask questions. There are two basic types of questions. The first type is known as a *yes / no* question because the answer that it is designed to elicit is either agreement *(yes)* or disagreement *(no)* (review Chapter 1).

Interrogative	Response
Is Alex looking for his dog?	*Yes, he is.*
Is she sleeping?	*No, she isn't.*
Does he always read at night?	*Yes, he does.*

2. If the main verb is *be*, put it at the beginning of the interrogative question:

Interrogative	Response
<u>Is</u> *John in the library?*	*No, he's at the movies.*
<u>Are</u> *they here?*	*Yes they are.*

3. If the verb is in a progressive tense, consisting of a "helping" verb and the present participle, put the helping verb at the beginning as well:

Interrogative	Response
<u>Is</u> *John <u>studying</u> in the library?*	*No, he's at the movies.*
<u>Are</u> *they <u>coming</u> soon?*	*Yes they are.*

4. If the verb is in a perfect tense, consisting of an *auxiliary* verb and the present participle, put the auxiliary verb at the beginning also:

Interrogative	Response
Has John gone to the library?	*No, he went to the movies.*
Have they arrived already?	*Yes they have.*

5. If the verb is a modal construction (Chapter 9), put the modal verb at the beginning of the sentence:

Interrogative	Response
Can he come to the concert as well?	*Yes, he can.*
Will she be going to Europe this fall?	*No, she will not.*

6. For all other kinds of verbs, use *do* (in the tense and mood of the main verb) at the beginning. The verb *do* is also called a helping verb:

Interrogative	Response
Does he always read at night?	*Yes, he does.*
Did she go to Europe last year?	*No, she did not.*

7. Here is a summary of the structure of *yes / no* questions:

If the verb is *be*:

Be	Subject	Rest of sentence
Is	she	here?
Are	they	Americans?

If the verb contains a participle:

Auxiliary / helping	Subject	Participle	Rest of sentence
Is	she	living	in Milwaukee?
Are	they	coming	to Chicago?
Has	he	played	that piece before?
Had	Mary	come	to the party?

If the verb contains a modal:

Modal	Subject	Verb	Rest of sentence
Can	*I*	*have*	*dessert?*
Will	*they*	*be coming*	*as well?*
Would	*you*	*mind*	*doing this for me?*
May	*I*	*suggest*	*something?*

For all other kinds of verbs:

Do	Subject	Infinitive	Rest of sentence
Does	*she*	*live*	*in Milwaukee?*
Do	*they*	*go*	*to Chicago often?*
Did	*he*	*study*	*for the exam?*
Did	*they*	*pass*	*the exam?*

8. Questions designed to seek approval, consent, agreement, or further information are called *tag questions* because they are formed with a "tag" at the end consisting of a helping verb or modal plus a pronoun:

    He is American, isn't he?
    We are always on time, aren't we?
    You like coffee, don't you?
    They haven't left, have they?
    They can come too, can't they?

9. Notice that a tag pronoun corresponds in person and number to the subject. The tag pronouns *it* (singular) and *they* (plural) are used when the subject contains a demonstrative, a quantifier, or an indefinite:

    This book is yours, isn't it?
    That is your laptop, isn't it?
    Everything is fine, isn't it?
    These things belong here, don't they?
    Those are your friends, aren't they?
    Many came late, didn't they?

10. If you wish to elicit an affirmative answer, use an affirmative sentence with a negative tag; however, if you wish to elicit a negative answer, use a negative sentence with an affirmative tag:

| | | **Affirmative** |
| **Affirmative sentence + negative tag** | **=** | **response** |

John is American, isn't he? — Yes, he is.
Your mother drives a van, doesn't she? — Yes, she does.
He used to work there, didn't he? — Yes, he did.
You're coming too, aren't you? — Yes, I am.

| | | **Negative** |
| **Negative Sentence + affirmative tag** | **=** | **response** |

John isn't American, is he? — No, he isn't.
Your mother does not drive a van, does she? — No, she doesn't.
He did not use to work there, did he? — No, he didn't.
You're not coming too, are you? — No, I am not.

11. Interrogative sentences can also be formed with *wh-* words that allow you to ask about content, information, and so on. They are called *wh-* words because they typically begin with the letters *wh* (except for *how, how about,* and so on). If you want information about something or someone, use these words:

What

What are you having for dinner?
What are these objects?
What college are you attending?
What does it matter?

How

How does this machine work?
How are you today?
How bad was it?
How is it that he left early?
How should I take that remark?
How's that again?

How about

How about a cup of tea?
How about going out tonight?

How come

How come you're so late?
How come you know so much?

Which

Which of these do you like?
Which part of town do you mean?

Who / whom

Who left
With whom did you go to the movies?
Who(m) did you see yesterday?

Where

Where is the telephone?
Where would we be without your help?
Where did you get this idea?
Where is this argument leading?

Why

Why is the door shut?

When

When will they be leaving?
Since when has this been going on?
Have they decided when they will be leaving for Europe?

Exercise Set 7-1

A. You are given a series of affirmative answers. Provide the questions that elicited each one.

1. Yes, he's here.
2. Yes, they're our relatives.
3. Yes, she's coming to Florida.
4. Yes, they're going to Europe.
5. Yes, he has heard that piece before.
6. Yes, they had come to the party.
7. Yes, you can have some coffee.
8. Yes, they'll be coming as well.
9. Yes, you may suggest something.
10. Yes, she goes to Harvard.
11. Yes, they go to Chicago often.
12. Yes, he passed the exam.
13. Yes, they understood my instructions.

B. Match the questions in the left-hand column with the responses in the right-hand column.

1. Where are they?
2. Who is he?
3. With whom did you go shopping?
4. Why did you shut the windows?
5. When will they be leaving?
6. Which purse do you prefer?
7. How about going out tonight?
8. How come you're so late?
9. How are you?
10. What is that?
11. They're coming as well, aren't they?
12. They're not coming too, are they?

(a) At four.
(b) Because it's cold outside.
(c) That one.
(d) A good friend.
(e) In Florida on vacation.
(f) Because I ran into heavy traffic.
(g) With my best friend.
(h) I'd like to, but I have to study.
(i) It's a new puzzle.
(j) Fine, thanks.
(k) No.
(l) Yes.

C.   Provide the appropriate tag pronoun that completes each question. Note that each question is supposed to elicit a *yes* response.

    1. She's American, isn't _____ ?
    2. They're always late, aren't _____ ?
    3. You study a lot, don't _____ ?
    4. He's here, isn't _____ ?
    5. They should come too, shouldn't _____ ?
    6. That CD is yours, isn't _____ ?
    7. Everything is OK, isn't _____ ?
    8. These belong here, don't _____ ?
    9. Those are your relatives, aren't _____ ?
    10. Many showed up late, didn't _____ ?

What Are Negatives?

1.   *Negatives* are words or expressions that allow you to deny, negate, contradict, refuse, or oppose something.

   I <u>do not</u> know anyone here.
   I <u>won't</u> do it anymore.
   You are <u>not</u> kind in saying that.

2.   Here is a summary of how to make sentences negative (review Chapter 1 as well):

   If the verb is *be,* simply put *not* or *-n't* (contracted form) after the verb:

Affirmative	**Negative**
She is here.	*She is not / isn't here.*
They are Americans.	*They are not / aren't Americans.*

   If the verb contains a present participle, put *not / -n't* after the helping verb *be:*

Affirmative	**Negative**
She is waiting for us.	*She is not / isn't waiting for us.*
They are watching TV.	*They are not / aren't watching TV.*
Mark was studying when you called.	*Mark was not / wasn't studying when you called.*

If the verb contains a past participle, put *not* / *-n't* after the auxiliary verb *have:*

Affirmative	Negative
He has played that before.	*He has not / hasn't played that before.*
They had come to the party too.	*They had not / hadn't come to the party.*

If the verb contains a modal, put *not* / *-n't* after the modal verb (the contracted form is not used with *may* and *might*):

Affirmative	Negative
I can eat dessert.	*I cannot / can't eat dessert.*
I might come too.	*I might not come.*
I would agree.	*I would not / wouldn't agree.*

For all other kinds of verbs, use *do* + *not* / *-n't* + *infinitive*, with *do* in the appropriate tense and mood.

Affirmative	Negative
She lives in Chicago.	*She does not / doesn't live in Chicago.*
They go to Florida often.	*They do not / don't go to Florida often.*
He studied for the exam.	*He did not / didn't study for the exam.*

3. To make a *yes* / *no* question negative, simply put *not* / *-n't* after the helping, auxiliary, or modal verb. Contractions are taken up in Chapter 15.

Helping / modal / auxiliary	Subject	Verb	Rest of sentence
Doesn't	*her mother*	*live*	*in Los Angeles?*
Don't	*they*	*live*	*in New York?*
Didn't	*Phil*	*study*	*for the exam?*
Didn't	*they*	*study*	*for the exam?*
Isn't	*that man*	*living*	*in Milwaukee?*
Aren't	*they*	*living*	*in Milwaukee?*
Won't	*he*	*be studying*	*for the exam?*
Can't	*Mary*	*come*	*to the party?*
Hasn't	*he*	*become*	*a lawyer?*
Hadn't	*she*	*decided*	*to practice medicine in Illinois?*

4. There is a more formal way of constructing negative questions. It involves putting *not* before the main verb:

Helping / modal / auxiliary	Subject	Verb	Rest of sentence
Does	*she*	*not live*	*in Milwaukee?*
Did	*he*	*not study*	*for the exam?*
Is	*she*	*not going*	*to Chicago?*
Can	*Mary*	*not come*	*to the party?*
Has	*Bill*	*not spoken*	*already?*

5. Recall from the above how affirmative and negative tag sentences are constructed. In addition, note that sentences with negative subjects take only affirmative tags:

Nothing is wrong, is it?
Nobody called, did they?

6. In some sentences, negative words other than *not* must be used in order for the sentence to make sense:

Affirmative	**Negative**
Everyone believes them.	*No one believes them.*
You always eat something.	*You never eat anything.*

7. The following are some common negative words:

never (opposite of *always*)

He had never been there before.
That will never do.

none (negative of *some*, *somebody*, and so on)

None dared to do it.
None of my classmates passed the exam.
That is none of your business.
He is none too ill.
The jeans looked none the better for having been washed.

neither (negative of *either, each,* and so on)

Neither shoe feels comfortable.
Neither the shoes nor the boots feel comfortable.
If he won't go, neither will she.

nothing (negative of *something, anything,* and so on)

The box contained nothing.
Nothing remains of the old house but the foundation.
The new policy means nothing to me.
They won by a score of two to nothing.
She looks nothing like her brother.

nobody (negative of *everybody, everyone,* and so on)

Nobody told you to go.
Nobody said that.

hardly (almost not)

I could hardly hear the speaker.

barely (by very little)

That is a barely furnished room.

rarely / seldom (not often)

I have rarely / seldom seen anything like it.

8. Negatives at the beginning of a sentence add emphasis. In this case, the subject and verb are inverted:

Never will I understand verbs!
Nobody, absolutely nobody, knows this!
Rarely have I seen something like this!

9. Finally, do not use double negatives:

Incorrect	Correct
Don't touch nothing!	*Don't touch anything!*
I never do nothing.	*I never do anything.*

Exercise Set 7-2

A. Make each sentence negative.

    1. He is an old friend.
    2. I was watching TV when you called.
    3. He has played that before.
    4. I would agree.
    5. He may come.
    6. Someone said that.
    7. She lives in France.
    8. He studied for the exam.
    9. Does his friend live in Los Angeles?
    10. Is Mary coming?
    11. Has he eaten yet?

B. Choose the appropriate negative word, (a) or (b).

    1. He had _____ done that before.
    (a) never
    (b) neither

    2. This is _____ of your business.
    (a) none
    (b) never

    3. If I don't go, _____ will he.
    (a) neither
    (b) nothing

    4. The box contained _____ .
    (a) nothing
    (b) anything

    5. The box did not contain _____ .
    (a) nothing
    (b) anything

6. _____ said that you should do that.
   (a) Nobody
   (b) Nothing

7. We could _____ hear the speaker.
   (a) barely
   (b) rarely

8. Nobody _____ that!
   (a) doesn't know
   (b) knows

9. Nothing is wrong, _____ ?
   (a) is it
   (b) isn't it

Negative Prefixes

1. There are several prefixes (elements attached to the beginning of words) that also allow you to negate something or to express its opposite. It is difficult to predict which one of them can be used with a specific word. You will simply have to observe them in context. Here are the most common ones:

a-

moral	→ *amoral*	not moral
historical	→ *ahistorical*	not historical

anti-

social	→ *antisocial*	against society
war	→ *antiwar*	against war

dis-

similar	→ *dissimilar*	not similar
interested	→ *disinterested*	not interested

Other Prefixes

Not all prefixes (of course) convey negation of some kind. Here are a few that do not:

auto- (of / by oneself): autobiography
bi- (two, twice): biannual, bilingual
ex- (former): ex-smoker, ex-boss
micro- (small): microwave
over- (too much): overdo, overwork
post- (after): postgraduate
pre- (before): precaution
pro- (in favor of): pro-labor
re- (again): reread, rewind
semi- (half): semiannual
sub- (under): subway, subdivision
under- (not enough): underpaid

in- (which becomes *il-* before *l*, *ir-* before *r*, and *im-* before *m*):

complete	→ incomplete	not complete
legal	→ illegal	not legal
regular	→ irregular	not regular
possible	→ impossible	not possible
moral	→ immoral	not moral

mis-

spell	→ misspell	spell incorrectly
inform	→ misinform	inform wrongly

non-

entity	→ nonentity	not an entity
combatant	→ noncombatant	not a combatant

pseudo-

intellectual	→ pseudointellectual	false intellectual
name	→ pseudonym	false (assumed) name

un-

happy	→ unhappy	not happy
healthy	→ unhealthy	not healthy
clean	→ unclean	not clean
ripe	→ unripe	not ripe

2. The suffix *-less* (added at the end) can also be used with some words. This conveys the idea of "lacking" or of "inability." Again, you will have to learn how to use this suffix through exposure and observation.

blame	→	blameless	without blame
rest	→	restless	incapable of staying still
penny	→	penniless	without money

Exercise Set 7-3

A. Give the equivalent for each using a word with a negative prefix or suffix.

1. without blame
2. not sure
3. assumed name
4. not an issue
5. inform wrongly
6. not moral
7. not probable
8. not responsible
9. not legal
10. not correct
11. not similar
12. not social

B. Now, give the equivalent for each using a word with a prefix.

1. not paid enough
2. twice annually
3. do something again
4. in favor of democracy
5. view beforehand
6. after the war
7. work too much
8. former schoolmate
9. biography of oneself

8

Verbs

You expect far too much of a first sentence. Think of it as analogous to a good country breakfast: What we want is something simple, but nourishing to the imagination. Hold the philosophy, hold the adjectives, just give us a plain subject and verb and perhaps a wholesome, nonfattening adverb or two.

Larry McMurtry (b. 1936)

The Simple Present

1. *Verbs* are words that indicate the action performed by the subject of a sentence. For this reason, they agree with the subject's person (first, second, third) and number (singular or plural).

You	*sing.*
↑	↑
2nd	2nd person singular

She	*sings.*
↑	↑
3rd	3rd person singular

2. In a dictionary, a verb is listed in its *infinitive* form. This is the form of the verb that is not marked for tense, person, and so on. It is the "default" form of the verb and may or may not be preceded by *to*:

read   or   *to read*
finish   or   *to finish*

3. The term *tense* indicates the time that an action occurred: *now* (present tense), *before* (past tense), or *after* (future tense). In this chapter, only the present and past tenses will be discussed. The future and conditional tenses will be taken up in the next chapter.

I'm eating it now (present tense).
I ate it yesterday (past tense).
I will eat it tomorrow (future tense).

The Simple Tenses

The *simple present* allows you to express actions that are permanent, habitual, usual, occurring, or about to occur in the near future *(I speak English, I always do that,* and so on). Its basic range of meaning encompasses the "now."

The *simple past,* also known as the *preterit,* allows you to talk about what began and ended in the past *(I spoke to her yesterday).* Its basic range of meaning encompasses the "before."

The *simple future* allows you to talk about things that will happen *(I will speak to him tomorrow).* Its basic range of meaning encompasses the "after."

4. Not only do verbs allow you to express a time relationship, but they also allow you to refer to the situation, to a point of view, and so on. This characteristic of verbs is known as *mood.*

   Mary is eating the sandwich (indicative mood or statement).

   Mary, eat that sandwich (imperative mood or command)!

   Mary may be eating that sandwich (probability).

5. A *regular verb* is one whose conjugation (the different forms it takes) follows a set pattern. A verb that does not is known as *irregular.* You will find common irregular verbs in the *Irregular Verbs* section.

6. As mentioned above, the *simple present* (also known as the *present indicative*) is the tense that allows you to refer to the "now" and to the "always." Regular verbs in the simple present undergo only one form—in the third-person singular an *-s* is added. Take, for example, the verb *speak:*

	Singular	**Plural**
first person	*I speak*	*we speak*
second person	*you speak*	*you speak*
third person (masculine)	*he speaks*	*they speak*
third person (feminine)	*she speaks*	*they speak*
third person (neuter)	*it speaks*	*they speak*

7. If the verb ends in *-y* and is preceded by a consonant, the third-person ending is spelled as *-ies:*

I try	but	*he tries*
they marry	but	*she marries*
we study	but	*he studies*
you reply	but	*she replies*

8. If the verb is preceded instead by a vowel, no spelling change is required:

I say	he says
you play	she plays
we stay	he stays
they buy	he buys

9. If the verb ends in *-o,* the third-person singular form is spelled with *-oes:*

I go	but	he goes
I do	but	she does

10. If the verb ends in *-s, -z, -sh, -ch,* or *-x,* add *-es:*

I fuss	but	he fusses
they fizz	but	it fizzes
you push	but	she pushes
we touch	but	he touches
they tax	but	he taxes

11. There are a number of irregular verbs in the simple present. Two frequently used ones are *be* and *have.* These verbs are important because they are also used as helping and auxiliary verbs. You can find other verbs in the *Irregular Verbs* section.

be

I am
you are
he / she / it is
we are
they are

have

I have
you have
he / she / it has
we have
they have

12. As discussed in the previous chapter, the negative forms of verbs in the simple present are constructed with *do + not / -n't + infinitive*:

Affirmative	**Negative**
I <u>love</u> apples.	I <u>do</u> <u>not</u> <u>love</u> apples.
He <u>sings</u> very well.	He <u>does</u> <u>not</u> <u>sing</u> very well.
My sister <u>likes</u> hockey.	My sister <u>does</u> <u>not</u> <u>like</u> hockey.
Their parents <u>live</u> in a	Their parents <u>do</u> <u>not</u> <u>live</u> in a
small house.	small house.

13. The interrogative form of the simple present is constructed with *do + subject + infinitive* (Chapter 7):

Affirmative	**Interrogative**
I <u>love</u> apples.	<u>Do</u> you <u>love</u> apples?
He <u>sings</u> very well.	<u>Does</u> he <u>sing</u> very well?
My sister <u>likes</u> hockey.	<u>Does</u> your sister <u>like</u> hockey?
Their parents <u>live</u> in a	<u>Do</u> their parents <u>live</u> in a
small house.	small house?

Exercise Set 8-1

A. Choose the correct form of the verb, (a) or (b).

1. He _____ English very well.
   (a) speak
   (b) speaks

2. They _____ fruit all the time.
   (a) eat
   (b) eats

3. I always _____ to do my best.
   (a) try
   (b) tries

4. Does he _____ often in class?
   (a) reply
   (b) replies

5. What instrument does he _____ ?
   (a) play
   (b) plays

6. How often does she _____ downtown?
   (a) go
   (b) goes

7. He always _____ what she tells him.
   (a) do
   (b) does

8. I _____ an American citizen.
   (a) is
   (b) am

9. She _____ a good friend.
   (a) are
   (b) is

10. They _____ lots of money.
    (a) have
    (b) has

11. That child _____ everything he sees.
    (a) touches
    (b) touch

12. I don't know why she _____ so much over everything!
    (a) fusses
    (b) fuss

B. Make each sentence negative.

1. He speaks English.
2. She has lots of money.
3. They go to Europe every year.
4. I play the piano.
5. He plays the cello.
6. My friends live in New York.

The Present Perfect

The Perfect Tenses

The *perfect* tenses allow you to say that something happened *before* something else.

Use the *present perfect* if the exact time is not important (*I have done it already*).

Use the *pluperfect*, also known as the *past perfect*, if the action was finished before another time in the past (*I had done it already when you arrived*).

Use the *future perfect* if the action will take place before another action in the future (*I will have already done it when they get here*).

The adverbs *ever, never, already, yet, still,* and *just* usually require the present perfect or pluperfect in the past:

> I haven't finished yet.
> She has never been to France.
> I had never heard that before.
> We had already eaten by one o'clock.

1. The *present perfect* tense allows you to refer to a past action that has been completed at the present time. It is a compound tense formed with the present tense of *have* and the past participle, in that order. *Have* is called the *auxiliary* verb:

    I <u>have</u> <u>eaten</u> already.
    Susan <u>has</u> <u>eaten</u> too.

2. To form the past participle of regular verbs, add *-ed* to the infinitive (called the *root*). If the infinitive ends in *-e*, just add *-d*:

Root (infinitive)	Past participle
shout	shouted
laugh	laughed
work	worked
return	returned
love	loved
dare	dared

4. If the infinitive contains a single syllable and ends in a single vowel + consonant, the consonant is doubled in the formation of the past participle:

Root (infinitive)	Past participle
stop	stopped
rub	rubbed
jam	jammed
fan	fanned
spot	spotted

5. If the ending is preceded by another consonant or more than one vowel, then doubling does not apply:

Root (infinitive)   **Past participle**

jump   *jumped*
learn   *learned*
rain   *rained*
fool   *fooled*

Syllables

A *syllable* is a unit of spoken language consisting of a single uninterrupted sound formed by a vowel or vowels followed or preceded by one or more consonants.

The word *play* has one syllable, but the word *playing* has two syllables: *play + ing*.

A stressed syllable is one that bears the main accent.

---

6. If the infinitive contains two syllables, doubling applies only if the second syllable is stressed:

First-syllable stress:

Root (infinitive)   **Past participle**

listen   *listened*
offer   *offered*
open   *opened*

Second-syllable stress:

Root (infinitive)   **Past participle**

prefer   *preferred*
control   *controlled*

7. If the infinitive root ends in *-y* and is preceded by a consonant, the past participle ending is written as *-ied*:

Root (infinitive)   **Past participle**

try   *tried*
cry   *cried*
worry   *worried*
study   *studied*

8. But if a vowel precedes the infinitive root, the -y is maintained:

Root (infinitive)	Past participle
play	*played*
enjoy	*enjoyed*
stay	*stayed*

9. There are many verbs whose past participles are not formed according to the above rules. Some of them are given below. Others can be found in the *Irregular Verbs* section:

Root (infinitive)	Past participle
be	*been*
do	*done*
eat	*eaten*
flee	*fled*
go	*gone*
have	*had*
hear	*heard*
read	*read*
say	*said*
see	*seen*
sing	*sung*
speak	*spoken*
take	*taken*

> **Pronunciation of -ed**
>
> If the final consonant of the root is "voiceless" *(k, p, s, f, sh, ch, ...)* the -ed sounds like -t: *looked = look + t.*
>
> If it is "voiced" *(g, b, z, v, ...)* the -ed sounds like -d: *cleaned = clean + d.*
>
> After *t* and *d* it is pronounced as -ed (with the -e sounding indistinct): *needed = need + ed.*

10. As you know by now, the negative form of the present perfect is constructed with *have + not / -n't + past participle* (Chapter 7):

Affirmative	Negative
I have spoken to her.	*I have not / haven't spoken to her.*
Alex has gone out.	*Alex has not / hasn't gone out.*
She has been there.	*She hasn't been there.*

11. The interrogative form of the present perfect is constructed with *have + subject + past participle* (Chapter 7):

Affirmative	Interrogative
I have spoken to her.	*Have you spoken to her?*
Alex has gone out.	*Has Alex gone out?*
She has been there.	*Has she been there?*

12. The present perfect, when used with *since* and *for*, allows you to refer to a situation that started in the past but which continues as you speak. Use *since* to indicate a starting point, which can be either a particular point in time or an action; use *for* if duration (number of years, days, and so on) is implied:

I have lived here since 1999.
I have lived here for twenty-one years.
They have known me since 2004.
They have known me for more than twenty-five years.
I have been studying English since I came to the United States.
They have been writing to us for a while.

Exercise Set 8-2

A.   Give the past participle of each verb.

1. play
2. care
3. learn
4. finish
5. eat
6. hear
7. flee
8. see
9. stop
10. jab
11. tan
12. rain
13. dump
14. open
15. refer
16. study
17. try
18. have
19. be
20. go

B. Change each verb into the present perfect. Follow the example.

Example: Mary eats the spaghetti / already.
          Mary has already eaten the spaghetti.

   1. The student studies / already.
   2. He does that / already.
   3. I take the bus / many times.
   4. She enjoys Beethoven's music / all her life.
   5. You stay with us / often.
   6. We learn to use good grammar / in school.

C. Turn each sentence into an interrogative one and negative one, changing the verb into the present perfect:

Example: She eats the pizza.
          Hasn't she eaten the pizza?

   1. He speaks to the professor.
   2. You do it.
   3. We say that.
   4. She takes it.
   5. They paint their house.

The Simple Past (Preterit)

   1. The *simple past,* also known as the *preterit,* allows you to refer to actions that occurred in the past without reference to the present.

   She played at Carnegie Hall last year.
   He came to the wedding late.
   I tried to contact them.
   We worked for that company many years ago.

2. The simple past is formed by adding *-ed* to the infinitive. Take, for example, *play*:

	Singular	**Plural**
first person	*I played*	*we played*
second person	*you played*	*you played*
third person (masculine)	*he played*	*they played*
third person (feminine)	*she played*	*they played*
third person (neuter)	*it played*	*they played*

3. The rules and features pertaining to the formation of past participles apply as well to the formation of the simple past. Review the section above if you have forgotten. For example, if the verb ends in *-e* just add *-d: love* → *loved.* Here is a brief summary of the other formation rules:

If the infinitive contains a single syllable and ends in a single vowel + consonant, the consonant is doubled in the formation of the simple past:

| *stop* | → | *stopped* |
| *spot* | → | *spotted* |

If the ending is preceded by another consonant or more than one vowel, doubling does not apply:

| *jump* | → | *jumped* |
| *learn* | → | *learned* |

If the infinitive contains two syllables, doubling applies only if the second syllable is stressed:

| *listen* | → | *listened* |
| *open* | → | *opened* |

but

| *prefer* | → | *preferred* |
| *control* | → | *controlled* |

If the infinitive root ends in *-y* and is preceded by a consonant, the simple past ending is written as *-ied*:

| *try* | → | *tried* |
| *study* | → | *studied* |

But if a vowel precedes the infinitive root, the -y is maintained:

play	→	*played*
stay	→	*stayed*

4. There are quite a number of irregular verbs in the simple past. You will simply have to learn them by memorizing. Some are given below, and others can be found in the *Irregular Verbs* section:

Root (infinitive)	**Simple past**
agree	*agreed*
come	*came*
do	*did*
eat	*ate*
flee	*fled*
go	*went*
have	*had*
hear	*heard*
read	*read*
say	*said*
see	*saw*
sing	*sang*
speak	*spoke*
take	*took*

5. Note the forms of *be* in the simple past:

I was
you were
he / she / it was
we were
they were

6. The negative form of the simple past is constructed with *did not / didn't + infinitive*:

Affirmative	**Negative**
I ate it.	*I did not / didn't eat it.*
He sang at the concert.	*He did not / didn't sing at the concert.*

7. The exception is the negative form of *be* in the simple past, which is constructed with *not / -n't* after the verb.

Affirmative

I was there.
We were angry.

Negative

I wasn't there.
We weren't angry.

8. The interrogative form of the simple past is constructed with *did not / didn't + subject + infinitive*:

Affirmative

I ate it.
He sang at the Met.

Interrogative

Did you eat it?
Did he sing at the Met?

9. Again, the exception is the *be*, which is constructed with *be* in the simple past put at the beginning of the sentence:

Affirmative

You were there.
He was angry.

Interrogative

Were you there?
Was he angry?

Exercise Set 8-3

A. Change each verb into the simple past.

Example: he sings
                  he sang

   1. I eat
   2. you are
   3. he has
   4. they are
   5. I am
   6. we are
   7. Mary is
   8. they see
   9. I take
   10. we hear

B.   Make each sentence negative.

1. We agreed with you.
2. She spoke to me.
3. He said that.
4. I heard it.
5. You went downtown.
6. He was late.
7. You were there.

C.   Make each sentence interrogative.

1. She saw you yesterday.
2. He had a toothache.
3. They did it already.
4. He was there too.
5. They were in the house yesterday.
6. He saw them too.
7. She sang a new tune.

The Pluperfect

1. The *pluperfect*, also known as the *past perfect*, is a compound tense. It is conjugated with the past tense of the auxiliary (*have*), which is *had*, and the past participle of the verb. If you have forgotten how to form the past participle, review the section above on the present perfect. The pluperfect allows you to express an action completed before a specified or implied past time. Simply put, it allows you to express an action that occurred *before* a simple past action:

> I <u>had eaten</u> already when you <u>arrived</u>.
>   ↑   ↑
> pluperfect   past

2. The negative form of the pluperfect is constructed with *had not / hadn't* + *past participle:*

Affirmative	**Negative**
I had spoken to her before.	*I had not / hadn't spoken to her before.*
Mike had gone out already.	*Mike had not / hadn't gone out.*
She had been there before.	*She had not / hadn't been there before.*

3. The interrogative form is constructed with *had* + *subject* + *past participle:*

Affirmative	**Interrogative**
I had spoken to her before.	*Had you spoken to her before?*
Mike had gone out already.	*Had Mike gone out already?*
She had been there already.	*Had she been there before?*

Exercise Set 8-4

A. Choose the appropriate form of the verb, (a) or (b).

1. When we arrived, the band _____ playing.
   (a) just finished
   (b) had just finished

2. While I _____ out yesterday, you called.
   (a) was
   (b) had been

3. It looks like she _____ before we arrived.
   (a) already sang
   (b) had already sung

4. Yes, he _____ it long before you called.
   (a) already did
   (b) had already done

5. We _____ to the store when you called.
   (a) went
   (b) had gone

B. Now, let's review all the verb tenses learned so far. Complete the chart with the missing forms of each verb.

	Simple present	Present perfect	Simple past	Pluperfect
reply	(he)	(I)	(she)	(we)
say	(he)	(I)	(she)	(we)
go	(he)	(I)	(she)	(we)
do	(he)	(I)	(she)	(we)
finish	(he)	(I)	(she)	(we)
reach	(he)	(I)	(she)	(we)
be	(he)	(I)	(she)	(we)
have	(he)	(I)	(she)	(we)
love	(he)	(I)	(she)	(we)
rub	(he)	(I)	(she)	(we)
gain	(he)	(I)	(she)	(we)
open	(he)	(I)	(she)	(we)
see	(he)	(I)	(she)	(we)
sing	(he)	(I)	(she)	(we)
speak	(he)	(I)	(she)	(we)
take	(he)	(I)	(she)	(we)

The Imperative

1. The *imperative* is the form of a verb that allows you to give commands, advice, directions, instructions, invitations, offers, prohibitions, and warnings and to make requests:

Think before you speak!
Eat all of it!
Don't do that!
Come to our get-together, OK?

2. The affirmative imperative is equivalent to the infinitive of the verb. Take, for instance, the verb *eat:*

Singular

Sarah, eat the orange!
Ms. Smith, try your best!

Plural

Alex and Sarah, eat the cherries!
Ladies and gentlemen, try your best!

3. The negative imperative is constructed with *do not / don't + infinitive*:

Affirmative

Sarah, <u>eat</u> the orange!
Girls, <u>drink</u> all your milk!
Boys, <u>be</u> nice!

Negative

Sarah, <u>do not / don't eat</u> the orange!
Girls, <u>do not / don't drink</u> soda pop!
Boys, <u>do not / don't be</u> naughty!

Exercise Set 8-5

A. Tell the following people to take the indicated actions.

> *Example:*   Tell Mark to eat all the pizza
> *Mark, eat all the pizza!*

Tell Mark ...

1. to drink all the milk.
2. to come early.
3. to be silent.
4. to speak English.

Tell Mr. and Mrs. Smith ...

5. to watch the new TV show.
6. to go out.
7. to finish the cake.

B. Now tell the same people not to do the indicated things.

> Example: Tell Mark not to eat all the pizza.
> *Mark, don't eat all the pizza!*

Tell Mark not ...

1. to drink all the milk.
2. to come early.
3. to be silent.
4. to speak English.

Tell Mr. and Mrs. Smith not ...

5. to watch the new TV show.
6. to go out.
7. to finish the cake.

The Progressive Tenses

1. The *progressive tenses* allow you to zero in on an action or condition in progress:

   I <u>am talking</u> to Mary right now.
   I <u>have been walking</u> all day.
   I <u>was walking</u> when I ran into him.
   I <u>will be going</u> to France next month.

2. The *present progressive* tense allows you to zero in on an ongoing action. In effect, it allows you to say that something is in progress as you speak. It is made up of the verb *be* in the present—*I am, you are, he / she / it is, we are, they are*—and the present participle of the verb, which is formed by adding *-ing* to the root (infinitive form): *watch → watching:*

   At this moment, she <u>is</u> <u>watching</u> TV.
   Don't distract him. He <u>is</u> <u>studying</u>.

> **The Progressive Tenses**
>
> These tenses are formed with *be* + *present participle.*
>
> They allow you to say that an action is in progress at a particular time, now, before, or after *(He is sleeping right now; He was sleeping when I got there; He will be sleeping when I arrive, as always).*
>
> The *perfect* forms of the progressive are constructed with *have* + *been* + *present participle.*
>
> These forms allow you to say that an action is in progress immediately before, or up to, another one *(He had been sleeping for two hours when I got there; He will have been sleeping for a long time by the time I get there).*

3. If the verb ends in *-e*, drop the vowel before adding *-ing:*

Root (infinitive)	**Present participle**
leave	*leaving*
have	*having*

Exceptions (if the ending is *-ee*):

see	*seeing*
flee	*fleeing*

4. If the infinitive contains a single syllable and ends in a single vowel + consonant, the consonant is doubled in the formation of the present participle:

Root (infinitive)	Present participle
stop	*stopping*
rub	*rubbing*
jam	*jamming*
fan	*fanning*
spot	*spotting*

5. If the infinitive is preceded by a consonant or more than one vowel, doubling does not apply:

Root (infinitive)	Present participle
jump	*jumping*
learn	*learning*
rain	*raining*
fool	*fooling*
dream	*dreaming*

6. If the infinitive contains two syllables, doubling applies only if the second syllable is stressed:

First-syllable stress:

Root (infinitive)	Present participle
listen	*listening*
offer	*offering*
open	*opening*

Second-syllable stress:

Root (infinitive)	Present participle
prefer	*preferring*
control	*controlling*

7. If the root ends in -*ie*, change the ending to -*y* before adding -*ing*:

Root (infinitive)	Present participle
lie	*lying*
tie	*tying*
vie	*vying*

8. Sometimes the present progressive is used in a time clause (a clause starting with *when, as soon as, after,* and so on) to express a future action or to convey the idea of a planned event:

   While I am traveling in France next year, I intend to visit the Louvre.
   I am seeing the dentist later today.
   After lunch, I am meeting with my professor.

9. As discussed in Chapter 7, the negative form of the present progressive is constructed simply by putting *not* before the present participle:

Affirmative	Negative
He *is studying* French.	He *is not / isn't studying* French.
They *are eating* lunch right now.	They *are not / aren't eating* lunch right now.

10. The interrogative form is constructed by putting the helping verb *be* at the beginning:

Affirmative	Negative
He *is studying* French.	*Is he studying* French?
They *are eating* lunch right now.	*Are they eating* lunch right now?

11. The *present perfect progressive* allows you to zero in on an action that has been ongoing with reference to the present. It is constructed with *have* + *been* + *present participle*:

    I have been walking for a while. And you?
    What has he been doing for the past hour?

Simple Present Versus Present Progressive

When speaking about actions, adverbs such as *always, forever,* and *constantly* (among many others) allow you to emphasize that the action is habitual:

> They *always* complain and *constantly* fuss.

The progressive is used with such adverbs when you want to complain or express annoyance or anger:

> She is *always* complaining and *constantly* fussing!

12. When used with *since* and *for*, the present perfect progressive allows you to express a situation that started in the past and continues on to the present time. Recall from above that if a particular point in time (a date, a day, and so on) is involved, you must use *since*; if time duration (number of years, days, and so on) is involved, you must use *for* instead

    I have been living here since 1999.
    I have been living here for twenty-one years.
    They have been playing in the symphony orchestra since 2004.
    They have been playing in the symphony orchestra for more than
        twenty-five years.

13. The negative form of the present perfect progressive is constructed simply by putting *not* before *been*:

Affirmative	**Negative**
He *has been studying* French for years.	He *hasn't been studying* French for years.
They *have been eating* lunch.	They *haven't been eating* lunch.

14. The interrogative form is constructed by putting the auxiliary verb at the beginning:

Affirmative	**Interrogative**
He has been studying French for years.	*Has he been studying* French for years?
They have been eating lunch.	*Have they been eating* lunch?

15. The *past progressive* allows you to zero in on an action that was ongoing with another one in the past. It is made up of the verb *be* in the simple past (preterit)—*I was, you were, he / she / it was, we were, they were*—and the present participle of the verb:

    My sister was eating yesterday when our aunt arrived.
    What were you doing yesterday when I phoned you?

16. The negative form is constructed simply by putting *not* before the present participle:

Affirmative	Negative
He *was studying* before.	He *was not / wasn't studying* before.
They *were eating* lunch.	They *were not / weren't eating* lunch.

17. The interrogative form is constructed by putting the auxiliary at the beginning:

Affirmative	Interrogative
He *was studying* before.	*Was he studying* before?
They *were eating* lunch.	*Were they eating* lunch?

18. To express actions that were incomplete, unfinished, or habitual in the past, you must use the simple past instead. The past progressive is not the English equivalent of the imperfect tense used in many other languages. The phrase *used to* followed by the infinitive can, however, be used as a substitute for the simple past to bring out the concept of "habitualness":

I *visited my grandparents regularly.*	or	I *used to visit my grandparents regularly.*
I *got up at five every morning.*	or	I *used to get up at five every morning.*

19. Stative verbs are rarely used in progressive tenses. It is incorrect to say something such as *I am liking this very much.* The only correct way is *I like it very much.* Similarly, the form *I am knowing what you are saying* is incorrect. The correct form is the simple present: *I know what you are saying.*

Stative Verbs

Some English verbs have a *stative meaning.* This means, simply, that they refer to states.

Common stative verbs are *like, seem, appear, look like, taste, smell, love, know, understand, believe, suppose, hate, prefer.* Some dictionaries will tell you if a verb is stative or not.

20. Some verbs have both stative and nonstative uses. One of these is *taste*:

Stative	**Nonstative**
He is always tasting the sauce while he cooks.	*It always tastes too spicy.*

21. Phrases constructed with *be + adjective* convey a stative meaning:

    I am sick today.
    She is nervous about her performance.

22. However, the progressive can be used to describe a temporary, ongoing situation:

    Alex is being rather quiet today, don't you think?
    She is being foolish. Ignore her!

    (*Note:* If you know Spanish, the stative uses correspond to the use of *estar*, and the nonstative uses to *ser*.)

> **Common Adjectives Used with *be + adjective***
>
> | | |
> |---|---|
> | bad | good |
> | logical | illogical |
> | cruel | fair |
> | unfair | funny |
> | lazy | kind |
> | careful | generous |
> | loud | rude |
> | noisy | serious |
> | quiet | polite |
> | impolite | patient |
> | foolish | nice |
> | silly | nervous |

23. Last, there is a *pluperfect progressive* tense that allows you to relate a past progressive action to another past action:

    She <u>had been studying</u> when you arrived.
    I <u>had been sleeping</u> when you phoned.

24. It is formed with *had been + present participle*. The negative is formed in the usual way, by putting *not* before *been*:

    She <u>had not / hadn't been studying</u> when you arrived.
    I <u>had not / hadn't been sleeping</u> when you phoned.

25. The interrogative is formed by putting *had* at the beginning:

    <u>Had she been studying</u> when you arrived?
    <u>Had you been sleeping</u> when I phoned?

Exercise Set 8-6

A. Fill in the chart with the appropriate progressive forms of the given verb.

	Present	Present perfect	Past	Pluperfect
lie	(he)	(I)	(she)	(we)
say	(he)	(I)	(she)	(we)
go	(he)	(I)	(she)	(we)
do	(he)	(I)	(she)	(we)
finish	(he)	(I)	(she)	(we)
reach	(he)	(I)	(she)	(we)
have	(he)	(I)	(she)	(we)
love	(he)	(I)	(she)	(we)
rub	(he)	(I)	(she)	(we)
gain	(he)	(I)	(she)	(we)
open	(he)	(I)	(she)	(we)
see	(he)	(I)	(she)	(we)
sing	(he)	(I)	(she)	(we)
speak	(he)	(I)	(she)	(we)
take	(he)	(I)	(she)	(we)

B. Choose the appropriate verb form, (a) or (b).

1. He _____ when you called.
   (a) has been sleeping
   (b) had been sleeping

2. He _____ rather foolish, don't you think?
   (a) is being
   (b) had been

3. She _____ how you play the piano.
   (a) is liking
   (b) likes

4. I _____ what you mean.
   (a) am knowing
   (b) know

5. They _____ when you arrived.
   (a) are studying
   (b) were studying

6. She _____ playing piano for years.
   (a) is
   (b) has been

Reflexive and Indefinite Verbs

1. A *reflexive* verb requires reflexive pronouns. More technically, it is a verb having an identical subject and direct object:

   <u>She</u> dressed <u>herself</u>.
   <u>I</u> have never enjoyed <u>myself</u> at the movies.

2. A reflexive infinitive can be identified by the ending *oneself*:

   (to) dress oneself
   (to) enjoy oneself

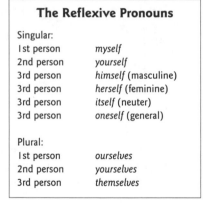

3. Reflexive verbs are conjugated and used in exactly the same manner as other verbs with, of course, reflexive pronouns. So there is nothing to be learned about them that you haven't already learned by studying the previous sections.

The Reflexive Pronouns	
Singular:	
1st person	*myself*
2nd person	*yourself*
3rd person	*himself* (masculine)
3rd person	*herself* (feminine)
3rd person	*itself* (neuter)
3rd person	*oneself* (general)
Plural:	
1st person	*ourselves*
2nd person	*yourselves*
3rd person	*themselves*

Please don't interrupt me; I am enjoying myself (present progressive).
They have been enjoying themselves for the past hour (present perfect progressive).

4. *Indefinite* tenses are verb forms that allow you to express actions that refer to indefinite time relations:

   Seeing is believing.
   To love is the purpose of life.

5. The *infinitive* is an indefinite verb form that can function as a substantive (a subject or predicate) while retaining certain verbal characteristics and is preceded by *to* unless the verb is a complex one (with a modal, for example):

To go willingly is to show strength.
We want him to work harder.

but

She couldn't read the letter.
We may finish today.

> **Adjective + infinitive**
>
> Certain adjectives can be followed by the infinitive. In general, these describe persons, not things, and especially their feelings or attitudes:
>
> *glad to (hear from you)*
> *happy to (help you out)*
> *certain to (succeed in life)*
> *careful to (do anything)*
> *eager to (please)*
> *ready to (learn a new language)*
> *proud to (see them succeed)*
> *lucky to (be so successful)*
> *pleased to (help them out)*
> *sorry to (hear he is retiring)*
> *afraid to (talk to them)*
> *upset to (do anything about it)*

---

6. An infinitive verb with an element, usually an adverb, interposed between *to* and the verb, as in *to boldly go*, is known as a split infinitive. The split infinitive has been present in English ever since the fourteenth century, but it was not until the nineteenth century that grammarians first labeled and condemned its usage. Today, however, it is generally well-tolerated.

7. When a verb follows another verb, the second one is either in the infinitive or the gerund form (see below). Common verbs followed by the infinitive are *hope, plan, intend, decide, promise, agree, seem, appear, ask, expect, need,* and *want.* In the negative, *not* is placed just before the infinitive:

   I hope to go to Italy next fall.
   They plan to renovate in the spring.
   She seems to know a lot.
   He promised not to be late.

8. Some verbs are followed by a noun or pronoun before the infinitive. These include *tell, advise, encourage, remind, invite, allow, warn, require, order, force,* and *ask:*

   I told Mary to watch that show.
   They advise us not to travel by bus.
   We invited our friends to come to dinner.
   She always requires her guests to take off their shoes.

9. There is also a *past infinitive* consisting of the auxiliary verb *have* and the past participle. It allows you to express an action that occurred before the time of some other action:

Present infinitive	Past infinitive
_To go_ willingly is _to show_ strength.	_To have gone_ willingly is _to have shown_ strength.
We want him _to work_ harder.	We wanted him _to have worked_ harder.

10. The _gerund_ is an indefinite verb form that can be used as a substantive (noun). It is formed exactly like the present participle (see the section above on the progressive tenses) and can be used as the subject or the object of a sentence (or a preposition):

Playing baseball can be fun.
We admired the choir's _singing_.
They are excited _about going_ to Russia.
I'm interested _in learning_ more about the ancient world.

11. In the negative form _not_ must precede the gerund:

They are upset about not going to Russia.
Not exercising can lead to health problems.

12. As you saw above, some verbs and expressions are followed by the infinitive. Others are instead followed by a preposition and a gerund. You will simply have to memorize each set:

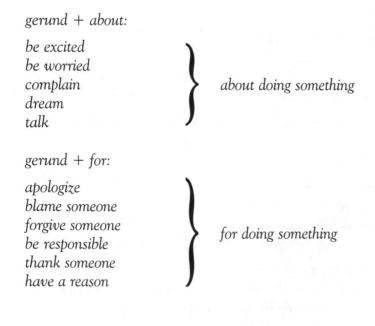

gerund + about:

be excited
be worried
complain
dream
talk

} about doing something

gerund + for:

apologize
blame someone
forgive someone
be responsible
thank someone
have a reason

} for doing something

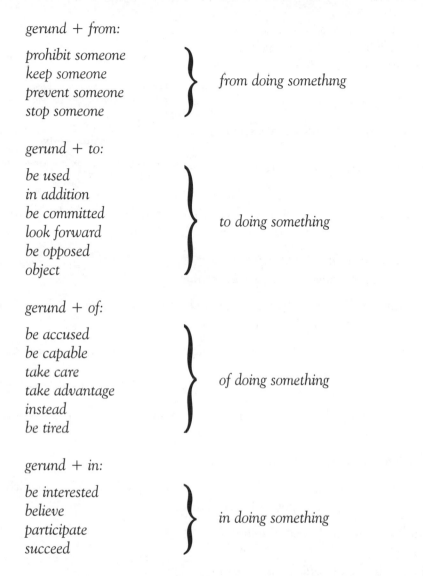

gerund + from:

prohibit someone
keep someone
prevent someone
stop someone

from doing something

gerund + to:

be used
in addition
be committed
look forward
be opposed
object

to doing something

gerund + of:

be accused
be capable
take care
take advantage
instead
be tired

of doing something

gerund + in:

be interested
believe
participate
succeed

in doing something

13. After verbs such as *enjoy, quit, stop, finish, avoid, consider, mention, go,* and *suggest,* only the gerund can be used:

I enjoy playing baseball.
He finishes working at seven.
They are considering joining a health club.
We always try to avoid saying unpleasant things.
We go fishing a lot.
They go shopping every Saturday.
They had difficulty finding our place.

14. There is also a *past gerund*, consisting of *having* + *past participle*. This allows you to indicate that something happened before the time of the main verb:

Having eaten everything, we went out.
Having learned English, we found many good jobs.

| **In Order** |
| This expression is used to convey purpose. It is followed by the infinitive: |
| *In order to learn English, you must study hard.* / *To learn English, you must study hard.* |
| **Perception Verbs** |
| *see, notice, watch, look at, observe, hear, listen to, feel, smell* |

15. Some verbs can be followed by either the infinitive or the gerund. These include *begin, like, start, continue, love, prefer, hate, can't stand:*

It started to rain. / *It started raining.*
I like to play tennis. / *I like playing tennis.*

16. Certain verbs of perception can also be followed by either the infinitive (in simple form) or the gerund:

I saw him run down the street yesterday. / *I saw him running down the street yesterday.*
I heard the rain fall on the roof. / *I heard the rain falling on the roof.*

17. An infinitive phrase used with *it* as the subject refers to the infinitive phrase itself:

It is impossible to learn English quickly.

18. If the phrase is put in the subject slot, *it* is deleted. In this case, either the infinitive or the gerund can be used:

To learn English quickly is impossible.
or
Learning English quickly is impossible.

Exercise Set 8-7

A. Correct the error in each sentence.

1. She always enjoys myself at the movies.
2. Are you enjoy yourself?
3. Go willingly is to show strength.
4. She hopes going to Spain next year.

5. I am lucky be so successful.
6. They wanted come early.
7. To go willingly is to have shown courage.
8. I am interested in learn more about grammar.
9. He always complains about to eat out.
10. You must forgive me for speak too candidly.
11. I am going to try to prevent you from to smoke.
12. We look forward to be with you.
13. I am tired of work so hard.
14. He has succeeded in to become rich.
15. She finished to work early today.
16. Eating everything, we decided to go out.
17. I saw him to walk down the street.
18. Is impossible to learn English quickly.

B. Make each sentence negative.

1. She not promised to be late.
2. You not seem to know much.
3. They are upset about going not to Europe.
4. Exercising not can lead to problems of health.
5. I would like to go not there.

9

Modal Verbs: the Future, the Conditional, and the Passive

Must! Is must a word to be addressed to princes? Little man, little man! thy father, if he had been alive, durst not have used that word.

Elizabeth I, Queen of England (1533–1603)

What Are Modal Verbs?

1. A *modal verb* is one of a set of verbs, including *can, could, may, might, must, ought, shall, should, will,* and *would,* that allow you to express or convey your attitude or mood:

   <u>Can</u> I come too?
   I <u>might</u> have to go away to college.
   I <u>would</u> like to buy a new computer.
   She <u>will</u> definitely come with us.

2. Here are the main meanings that each modal allows you to express:

   can

   to indicate physical or mental ability:

   I can carry both suitcases.
   I cannot do that.

   to indicate possession of a specified privilege or skill:

   The president can veto congressional bills.
   I can tune pianos.

to indicate possibility or probability:

*I wonder if my long lost cat can still
  be alive.*

**to indicate that which is permitted
or to request permission:**

*One can hardly blame you for being
  upset.*
Can I be excused?

could (past tense of can)

**to indicate ability or possibility
in the past:**

I could run faster years ago.

Features

Modals do not take an -s ending when the subject is *he, she, one,* or *it:*

  She can do it.   not   *She cans do it.*

Modals are followed by the infinitive form of a verb without *to:*

  She can do it.   not   *She can to do it.*

The exception is *ought,* which must be followed by *to:*

  She ought to do it.

Modals cannot be followed by a verb in any other tense:

  He can come.   not   *He can came.*

---

to express hypothetical or conditional ideas:

If we could help, we would.

to express tentativeness or convey politeness:

Could you come over here?

may

to request or grant permission:

May I go swimming? Yes, you may.

to indicate a certain measure of likelihood or possibility:

It may rain this afternoon.

to express a desire or fervent wish:

Long may he live!

to express result (introduced by *so that*):

He wrote it so that the average person may understand.

(Note: This is true for other modals.)

I set the alarm so that I wouldn't oversleep this morning.

might (past tense of *may*)

to indicate a condition or state contrary to fact:

She might help if she knew the truth.

to indicate a weaker possibility than *may*:

We hope that we might discover a pot of gold.
She told him yesterday he might not go on the trip.

to express a high degree of politeness:

Might I express my opinion?

must

to express obligation, necessity, or requirement:

Citizens must register in order to vote.
Plants must have oxygen in order to live.

to express a command, an admonition, or a determination:

You simply must be careful.
If you must leave, do it quietly.

to indicate inevitability or certainty:

We all must die.

ought

to convey obligation, duty, advisability, or desirability:

You ought to work harder than that.
You ought to wear a raincoat.
You ought to have been there; it was great fun.

to indicate probability or likelihood:

She ought to finish by next week.

had better

can be used in place of *ought to* in implying negative consequences
if action is not taken:

We had better go before the storm becomes worse.

shall

to indicate that something will take place or exist in the future:

We shall arrive tomorrow.
That day shall come.

to indicate an order or an obligation:

They shall answer for their misdeeds.

(in question form) to make suggestions:

Shall we go?

should (past tense of shall)

to express obligation or duty:

You should send her a note.

to express probability, improbability, or expectation:

They should arrive at noon.
If she should fall, then so would I.

to moderate the directness of a statement:

I should think he would like to go.

will

to indicate future actions:

They will appear later.
You will regret this.
Will you help me with this homework?

to indicate requirement or command:

You will report to me afterward.

to indicate customary or habitual actions, capacities, and so on:

People will talk.
This metal will not crack under heavy pressure.

to indicate probability or expectation:

That will be the messenger ringing.

would (past tense of will)

to indicate request, desire, or preference:

I wish you would stay longer.
Would you go with me?
I would rather do it myself.

to indicate uncertainty:

It would seem to be getting warmer.

to indicate repeated past actions:

He would do it often.

to indicate unreal conditions:

If I had a million dollars, I would travel around the world.

3. *Phrasal modals* are modal constructions whose meanings are similar to those of some single modals. Unlike one-word modals, they show agreement between the subject and the verb as well as tense.

be able to (can)

I am indeed able to tune pianos.   or   *I can indeed tune pianos.*

be going to (will)

You are going to regret this.   or   *You will regret this.*

have to / have got to (ought to, must, should)

You simply have to study more.   or   *You simply must study more.*
He has got to work more on his technique.   or   *He should work more on his technique.*

4. To form a compound modal tense, use *modal + have + past participle:*
I should have gone to see that movie, but I had no time.
He may have already done it.
I could not have done it anyway.

5. The negative of modal constructions is formed by inserting *not* after the modal:

He may not know what is going on.
They will not be coming to the party.
I should not have gone to see that movie.
He may not have done it.

6. Note the following peculiar contractions:

cannot   →   *can't*
will not   →   *won't*

7. Do not contract the modals *may* and *shall* with *not*:

may not	not	*mayn't*
shall not	not	*shalln't*

8. The present progressive form of the modal is *modal + be + present participle*. It allows you to say that something is ongoing:

He may be sleeping, so do not call at this time.
She must be playing Beethoven. Who else could it be?

9. The past progressive form is *modal + have been + present participle*. It allows you to say that something was ongoing in the past:

He may have been sleeping when I called.
She must have been playing Beethoven. Who else could it have been?

10. For the use of modals in discourse to express politeness, necessity, advisability, expectations, and suggestions, see Chapter 13.

Exercise Set 9-1

A. Correct the error in each sentence.

1. He cans do it too.
2. Should I be excused?
3. I can run faster when I was younger.
4. If we should help, we would.
5. Would I come in?
6. Long should they live!
7. She said yesterday that they had not go on the trip.
8. Trees can have oxygen in order to survive.
9. If you can leave, do it quietly.
10. They willn't come till much later.
11. You mayn't do that.
12. I should gone to the mall with you.
13. He may sleep, so do not bother him.
14. He must play Chopin. Who else could it have been?

B.   Choose the appropriate form of the verb, (a) or (b).

    1. I _____ play the violin.
      (a) can
      (b) have

    2. I wonder if my long lost dog _____ still be alive.
      (a) can
      (b) would

    3. _____ I go out to play?
      (a) Had better
      (b) May

    4. You _____ come; it was great fun.
      (a) ought to have
      (b) ought to

    5. _____ we go? It's getting late.
      (a) Shall
      (b) Will

    6. If you _____ go to Europe, so would I.
      (a) should
      (b) could

    7. You are _____ like their house very much.
      (a) going to
      (b) able to

    8. You simply _____ work harder at it!
      (a) are going to
      (b) have to

The Future and the Conditional

1. The *simple future*, as its name implies, allows you to express an action that will occur in the future. It is formed with the modal verb *will* + *infinitive*:

   I <u>will go</u> away to college next year.
   She <u>will not go</u> to Europe after all.

2. Recall that *will not* is contracted to *won't* (*She won't go to Europe after all*). Moreover, *will* itself can be contracted to *-'ll*:

   I'll go away to college next year.
   She'll not go to Europe after all.

3. There is also a progressive form of the future that allows you to express an action that will be ongoing at a time in the future. It is formed with *will be* + *present participle*:

   She'll be traveling around Mexico next year.
   I will probably be studying when you arrive.

> **The Simple Future Versus *be going to***
>
> If you want to make a prediction, use either the simple future or the phrasal verb *be going to*:
>
> *It will be raining tomorrow.*
> *It is going to rain tomorrow.*
>
> *Be careful! You'll fall!*
> *Be careful! You're going to fall!*
>
> If you have a prior plan in mind, however, you can use only *be going to*:
>
> *I'm tired of going by bus. I am going to get a car at last.*
>
> If probability is involved, either one can be used:
>
> *I will probably buy a car.*
> *I am probably going to buy a car.*

4. The progressive form of *be going to* can be used as well (*be going to* + *be* + *present participle*):

   She is going to be moving next year.
   I am probably going to be studying when you arrive.

5. The *future perfect* tense allows you to relate a future action to another one as having occurred before it. It is formed with the *will have* + *past participle* (see Chapter 8):

   By the time you finish your part, I will have already finished mine.

6. Neither the future (simple or perfect) nor *be going to* (see sidebar on page 168) can be used in a time clause even though the main clause verb may be in the future:

> *After I get home, we will go out together.*
> *As soon as she arrives, we'll start the party.*
> *We will have eaten before he arrives.*
> *By the time he arrives, we will have eaten.*
> *Until she shows up, we are not going to do it.*
> *I'll never speak to her again as long as I live.*
> *When he decides to come, we will go out.*

Time Clauses

A *time clause* is a subordinate clause (see Chapter 1) formed with a temporal conjunction (*when, after, by the time,* and so on):

> When the phone rang, I was taking a shower.

The order of the time clause with respect to the main clause does not matter. However, if the main clause is put first, do not use a comma (as above):

> I was taking a shower when the phone rang.

7. The *conditional,* as its name implies, allows you to express a condition. It is formed with the modal *would + infinitive, could + infinitive,* and *might + infinitive.*

> *I would go away to college next year, but I don't have enough money.*
> *She would not go to Europe if she had her way.*
> *They could do it if they wanted.*
> *He might not come if you are not there.*

8. Notice that *would not* can be contracted to *wouldn't* (*She wouldn't go to Europe, if she had her way*).

9. The progressive form of the conditional allows you to express a condition that is in progress. It is formed with *would be + present participle:*

> *He would be studying French at this time, if I'm not mistaken.*
> *She would not be going to Europe if she had her way.*

10. The *conditional perfect* tense is formed with *would have + past participle* (see Chapter 8). It allows you to relate a conditional action to another one as having occurred before it, or to relate two conditional actions that took place at the same time:

> *She would have gone after you but forgot to do so.*
> *She would have gone to see that movie, but she was very busy.*

11. In some *if*-clauses, the simple present, past, or past perfect are used together with the future, the conditional, or some other modal construction in the main clause:

If I have enough time, I will watch that program.
If I had enough time, I would watch that program.
If I had had enough time, I would have watched that program.
If it rains, you should stay inside.
If it snows heavily, we can't go shopping.

Exercise Set 9-2

A. Complete the following sentences with *will* or *would*, as the case may be.

1. After you get home, we _____ have dinner.
2. As soon as he arrives, we _____ turn on the TV.
3. We _____ have eaten by the time he arrives.
4. I _____ go away to college next year, but I don't have enough money.
5. She _____ not go to that school if she had her way.
6. She _____ have gone to see that movie, but she was very busy.
7. I _____ definitely go with you to the movies tomorrow.
8. I _____ like to go with you, but I have no time.

B. Choose the correct form of the verb, (a) or (b).

1. If it _____, you should stay inside.
   (a) snows
   (b) snowed

2. If I _____ enough money, I would have bought a Mercedes.
   (a) have
   (b) had had

3. If I _____ enough time, I will go out with you.
   (a) have
   (b) had

4. I _____ like that very much.
  (a) would
  (b) would have

5. I _____ liked that very much.
  (a) would
  (b) would have

The Passive Voice

1. In this and the previous chapter, we have been dealing with verbs in the *active voice*. These are verbs that occur in sentences in which the subject of the sentence is performing or causing the action expressed by the verb. Now we will turn our attention to sentences in which the verb indicates that the grammatical subject is the object of the action or the effect of the verb:

Active	Passive
Alex eats the apple.	*The apple is eaten by Alex.*
Sarah already drank the milk.	*The milk was already drunk by Sarah.*

2. Any transitive active verb can be turned into a corresponding passive form (as discussed in Chapter 1). This can be done as follows:

    Change the order of the subject and the object:

    Alexander ate the apples. → *The apples ... Alexander.*

    Change the verb into the passive form by introducing the auxiliary verb *be* in the tense of the main verb and changing the latter into a past participle. Do not forget to make the passive verb agree with the subject:

    The apples ... Alexander. → *The apples were eaten ... Alexander.*

    Put *by* in front of the object (the previous active subject):

    The apples were eaten ... Alexander. → *The apples were eaten by Alexander.*

3. This three-part rule applies to any verb in any tense. Note that you must make appropriate changes to pronouns when they are changed from subject to object forms (Chapter 5):

Active	Passive
She will eat it.	*It will be eaten by her.*
I had eaten it.	*It had been eaten by me.*

4. The passive voice allows you to put the focus on the object. In some cases, it is an important element of style. For example, it should be used in technical and scientific discourse and to express generalities. In such cases, a generic passive applies, which is formed without the *by* phrase:

The experiment was conducted yesterday.
His writing was not appreciated.
The law has been misapplied.
Apples are eaten to improve health.

5. The passive without the *by phrase* is also used when it is not known (or not important to know) who or what performs an action:

Corn is grown in Indiana.
All our olive oil was imported from Italy.

6. The *by phrase* is inserted, however, if it is important to know who or what performs an action.

That poem was written by Emily Dickenson.
That dress was made by your tailor.

Examples of the Passives

In the examples below the active voice of the sentence is given first, followed by its corresponding passive form just below:

Simple present:
Alex *helps* her.
She *is helped* by Alex.

Present progressive:
Alex *is helping* her.
She *is being helped* by Alex.

Present perfect:
Alex *has helped* her.
She *has been helped* by Alex.

Simple past:
Alex *helped* her.
She *was helped* by Alex.

Past progressive:
Alex *was helping* her.
She *was being helped* by Alex.

Pluperfect:
Alex *had helped* her.
She *had been helped* by Alex.

Simple future:
Alex *will help* her.
She *will be helped* by Alex.

Future perfect:
Alex *will have helped* her.
She *will have been helped* by Alex.

Conditional:
Alex *would help* her, but ....
She *would be helped* by Alex, but ....

Conditional perfect:
Alex *would have helped* her, but ....
She *would have been helped* by Alex, but ....

7. There are only two forms of the modal passive:

   modal + be + past participle (present form)
   modal + have been + past participle (past form)

   He will be invited to the party by his friends.
   He should have been invited to the party, but he wasn't.
   Math should be taught to a child early on.
   That house must have been built in the 1950s.

8. There is also a stative form (see Chapter 8). In this case the *by phrase* cannot be used and the past participle functions as an adjective:

   The class is finished.
   She is married.
   The door is not locked.
   I am done with my work.

9. Many stative verbs are followed by prepositions:

   to

   He is engaged to Sara.
   I was exposed to that philosophy many years ago.
   That course is limited to only introductory topics.
   She is married to a very nice man.
   I am addicted to sitcoms.
   We are not connected to the Internet yet.
   That book is dedicated to his grandchildren.
   She is related to my colleague.

   with

   My stereo system is equipped with new technologies.
   I am finished with that work.
   He is filled with joy.
   I am not acquainted with them.
   She is done with all that work.

   from

   They are gone from our street.
   We are protected from danger.

about

I am concerned about the present state of affairs.
Are you worried about that as well?

in

I am involved in art.

10. There are also passive forms of infinitives and gerunds:

Active	**Passive**
to be + past participle	*to have been + past participle*
being + past participle	*having been + past participle*
I did not expect to be promoted.	*I was fortunate to have been promoted.*
I did not expect being promoted.	*Having been promoted did not change my life very much.*

Exercise Set 9-3

A. Make each sentence passive.

    1. Alex loves her.
    2. My friend is reading that novel.
    3. I have done it already.
    4. Mary called her.
    5. They were singing my favorite song.
    6. We had helped her.
    7. I will teach you.
    8. Your friends will have called her already.

B. Choose the appropriate verb form, (a) or (b).

    1. You were fortunate _____ promoted.
      (a) to have
      (b) to have been

2. His help was not _____ .
   (a) appreciated
   (b) appreciating

3. The law _____ wrongly applied in this case.
   (a) has
   (b) has been

4. She will also _____ to the party by us.
   (a) be invited
   (b) has been invited

5. That plaza _____ built in the 1960s.
   (a) must be
   (b) must have been

6. The door _____ not locked.
   (a) has
   (b) was

C.   Supply the missing preposition.

1. Jack is married _____ Julie.
2. I was exposed _____ that idea many years ago.
3. They are related _____ my brother-in-law.
4. I am filled _____ joy.
5. She is done _____ working late.
6. It is always best to protect your family _____ danger.
7. Are you worried _____ your health?
8. Are you involved _____ music?

── 10 ──

Phrasal and Idiomatic Verbs

*By such innovations are languages enriched, when the
words are adopted by the multitude, and naturalized by custom.*

Miguel de Cervantes (1547–1616)

What Are Phrasal and Idiomatic Verbs?

1. A *phrasal verb* or *construction* consists of a verb followed by one or
   more words (prepositions, adverbs, and so on) acting as a single verb
   unit. It is a verb unit, consisting of a verb and another word or
   words, with a single meaning.

   She <u>looked up</u> the word in the dictionary.
   He <u>got by</u> on a meager salary.

2. An *idiomatic expression* or *construction* is a combination of words fixed
   in form whose meaning cannot be determined by the separate meanings of the words in it. For example, the English expression *He kicked
   the bucket* for *He died* cannot be understood as the sum of the meanings of its separate words. Moreover, it cannot be altered in any way;
   otherwise it would lose its idiomatic meaning (*He kicks the buckets*;
   He kicks a bucket; and so on).

3. There is no magical formula for learning phrasal and idiomatic constructions. You will simply have to memorize them. Take, for example, *make* as used in the following constructions, some of which are
   phrasal and others idiomatic. As you can see, you will simply have
   to learn how to use them by observation and by consulting a good
   dictionary.

   make for

   That approach makes for better communication.

make off

He made off in a hurry upon seeing her arrive.

make out

I could barely make out the traffic signs.
I made out the invoices yesterday.
He made out well in business.
They made out in the back seat of the car.

make over

You need to make over that bedroom.

Make
Simple past:
(I) made, (you) made, (he) made, (she) made, (we) made, (they) made
Present participle:
making
Past participle:
made

make up

The pharmacist made up a new prescription.
She made up her face before going out.
We made up the difference in the bill.
They kissed and made up.

make a clean breast of

If you make a clean breast of the past, you can go forward.

make a face

She made an awful face at me.

make a go of

They have made a go of the business.

make away with

The thief made away with quite a bit of money.

make believe

You have to make believe that you are strong in order to win.

make do

They had to make do on less income.

make ends meet

You'll have to make ends meet with what you have.

make eyes

The two young people made eyes at each other.

make fun of

Do not make fun of me!

make good

He made good his escape.

make it

She finally made it as an actor.

make light of

He made light of his illness.

make love / war

It is better to make love than war.

make off with

He made off with the profits.

make the scene

He made the scene at the party.

make up (one's) mind

I don't know which one to choose; I haven't made up my mind yet.

make way

Make way for him.

4. This verb can also be used as a *causative*—a verb form that allows you to express the idea: "*X causes / forces Y to do something.*" It is followed by the simple infinitive (the infinitive without *to*):

She made her brother wash the dishes.
I will make you regret your words.
Sad movies make him cry.
The mother made her daughter clean her room.

5. The verb *have* can be used in place of *make*, in some cases. So can *get*, which must be followed by a complete infinitive:

She had her brother wash the dishes.
The mother had her daughter clean her room.

She got her brother to wash the dishes.
The mother got her daughter to clean her room.

Exercise Set 10-1

A. Fill in the blanks with the missing part of the phrasal or idiomatic construction.

1. Your style has always made _____ better communication.
2. They made _____ in a hurry upon seeing us arrive.
3. You need to make _____ that room.
4. Get your doctor to make you _____ a new prescription.
5. Why do you make _____ your face so much when you go out on a date?
6. Let's kiss and make _____ , OK?
7. Why do you always make those awful _____ when I talk to you?
8. The robbers made _____ with a lot of money.
9. We're going to have to make _____ on less money.
10. We are always trying to make ends meet _____ what we have.
11. I caught them making eyes _____ each other.
12. Why are you always making _____ of me?
13. He finally made _____ as a successful musician.

14. Do not make _____ of our situation!
15. They made _____ with the profits.
16. Have you made _____ your mind yet?

B. Match the parts in the columns to make complete sentences.

1. I had my brother   (a) her to clean her room.
2. Her parents got   (b) him tidy up the garage.
3. We had   (c) got me to look up the new words.
4. My teacher   (d) wash the dishes.
5. They got us   (e) to reconsider.

Constructions with *Do* and *Go*

1. Most of the phrasal verbs and idiomatic constructions in English are constructed with frequently used verbs such as *do*, *go*, and *get*.

   He cannot do without sports.
   I try to get by on little money.

2. Here are some common phrasal and idiomatic constructions with *do* and *go*. You can use this list as a point of reference:

do by

The children have done well by their poor parents.

do for

I will do for you what I have always done.

do in

The marathon did me in.
Huge losses on the stock market did us in.

Do and Go

Do

Simple present:

(I) do, (you) do, (he) does, (she) does, (we) do, (they) do

Simple past:

(I) did, (you) did, (he) did, (she) did, (we) did, (they) did

Past participle:

done

Go

Simple present:

(I) go, (you) go, (he) goes, (she) goes, (we) go, (they) go

Simple past (preterit):

(I) went, (you) went, (he) went, (she) went, (we) went, (they) went

Past participle:

gone

do up

The children were all done up in matching outfits.
Do up the buttons on your dress!

do without

There was no television on the island, but we soon learned to do without.

do away with

We did away with that subscription. The magazine was too expensive.

do (one) proud

He always does us proud.

do (one's) bit

You must do your bit! I cannot do everything myself!

do (one's) own thing

She always does her own thing. She's a true individualist.

go about

Go about your chores in a responsible way!

go along

They will go along with anything you want to do.

go around

There's just enough food to go around.
Many rumors are going around.

go at

He went at the job with a lot of energy.

go by

As time goes by, you realize that many things are not important.
My parents were away when we went by last week.

go down

The sun went down.
How will your ideas go down at the meeting?

go for

I really go for progressive jazz.
He's an opponent who is known to go for the jugular in arguments.

go in

She went in with the others to buy a present.

go off

The siren went off at noon.
The project went off smoothly.

go on

She didn't know what was going on.
Don't go on talking and talking!

go out

He went out at seven.
High boots went out last year.

go over

That new style just didn't go over.
Go over the test scores and you'll see a pattern.

go through

He went through the students' papers.
I went through the sonata in thirty minutes.

go under

That business went under because of poor management.

go with

My brother has been going with your sister for a while, correct?

go back on

You should not go back on a promise.

go belly up

A record number of companies went belly up last year.

go by the board

Old dress codes have now gone by the board. Nobody likes them.

go for broke

Why not go for broke and start our own business?

go in for

He goes in for classical music.

go it alone

You must go it alone to be truly independent!

go off the deep end

Don't go off the deep end and make a scene!

go out of (one's) way

He always goes out of his way for others.

go out the window

That theory went out the window years ago. Nobody even remembers it.

go places

She's a young executive who is clearly going places.

go steady

They have been going steady for seven years. Now, they intend to marry.

go without saying

It goes without saying that success is the product of hard work.

Exercise Set 10-2

A. Fill in the blanks with the missing parts of the constructions consisting of the verb *do*.

1. They have done _____ by their friends.
2. I will do _____ him what I have done for you.
3. Huge losses on the stock market did them _____ .
4. Do _____ the buttons on your shirt!
5. I cannot do _____ TV at night.
6. We did away _____ that TV set because it was getting old.
7. She does us _____ because she is such a good person.
8. Everyone must do their _____ ; otherwise it would not be fair.
9. He always does his own _____ ; no matter who is with him.

B. Now, fill in the blanks with the missing parts of the constructions consisting of the verb *go*.

1. You must go _____ your chores in a responsible way!
2. I will not go _____ with anything you want to do.
3. There's not enough food to go _____ .

4. They went _____ the job with a lot of energy.
5. As the years go _____ , I am becoming wiser.
6. How do you think my proposal will go _____ at the meeting?
7. I really go _____ the music of Beethoven.
8. His projects always go _____ smoothly.
9. Can you tell me what is going _____ ?
10. At what time do you want to go _____ ?
11. Go _____ the list and you'll see a pattern.
12. You should never go back _____ a promise.
13. A record number of retail stores went belly _____ last year.
14. Why not go for _____ and start our own business?
15. Do you go _____ classical music?
16. To be truly independent, you must go _____ alone.
17. I always go _____ of my way for you.
18. She is someone who is clearly going _____ .
19. For how long have they been going _____ ?
20. It goes _____ saying that success is hard to come by without hard work.

Constructions with *Look, Have,* and *Stay*

1. Three other common verbs used in many phrasal and idiomatic constructions are *look, have,* and *stay.*

2. Here are some common constructions with these verbs.

look after

She looks after her younger brother.

look for

Look for a change of weather in March.

look on or upon

We looked on them, mistakenly, as incompetents.

look out

If you don't look out, you may fall on the ice.

look up

Look it up in an encyclopedia.
Things are at last looking up.

look a gift horse in the mouth

Never look a gift horse in the mouth.
* Be happy with what you get.*

look alive

Look alive! We leave in five minutes.

Have

Simple present:

  (I) have, (you) have, (he) has, (she) has, (we) have, (they) have

Simple past (preterit):

  (I) had, (you) had, (he) had, (she) had, (we) had, (they) had

Present participle:

  having

Past participle:

  had

---

look down on or look down upon

They look down on our efforts all the time, no matter how much we try.

look forward to

They're looking forward to graduation.

look sharp

Your new pants make you look really sharp.

look up to

The promising young poet looked up to the older poet.

have on

She had on red shoes.
We have a dinner party on for tomorrow evening.

have had it

That coat has had it. It is time to get a new one.

have it in for (someone)

He has it in for me, so I'm trying to avoid him.

have it out

Okay, let's have it all out between you and me. Let's settle this once and for all.

have (something) coming

You have had that reprimand coming for a very long time.

have to do with

Your remark has nothing to do with what I'm saying.

stay put

For the present time, just stay put and don't get out of bed!

stay the course

To succeed, one must stay the course and never give up!

Exercise Set 10-3

A. Which verb fits in each blank, *have* or *stay*? Provide the appropriate verb in its correct form.

1. She _____ on new shoes yesterday.
2. Mary, _____ the course, otherwise you won't succeed!
3. We _____ a wedding party to go to tomorrow evening.
4. That car has _____ it. It is time to get a new one.
5. I know that my boss _____ it in for me, so I'm trying to avoid him.
6. Okay, let's _____ it all out between the two of us. This is getting ridiculous.
7. You _____ that scolding coming for a long time.
8. What you just said _____ nothing to do with what I'm saying.
9. For now, just _____ put and don't go out with her!

B. Fill in the blanks with the missing parts of the constructions consist-
    ing of the verb *look*.

    1. I looked _____ her, mistakenly, as being on the other side.
    2. If I don't look _____ , I may fall on the ice.
    3. Where should I look you _____ ?
    4. Look _____ ! We are about to have some fun.
    5. Don't be always looking _____ on my work, please!
    6. We're looking _____ to spending some time together.
    7. Your new shoes make you look really _____ .
    8. I have always looked _____ to my teachers.

Constructions with Get

1. The most troublesome phrasal verb for the ESL student is undoubt-
    edly *get* because it is so uniquely characteristic of English usage—
    more so than any other verb in the language.

2. Here are some common phrasal and idiomatic constructions made
    up with this verb.

get about

It's hard to get about in a wheelchair.

get across

*I have tried to get my point across over
    and over.*
How can I get across to the students?

Get
Simple past:
(I) got, (you) got, (he / she / it) got, (we) got, (they) got
Present participle:
getting
Past participle:
got / gotten

get after

You should get after them to mow the lawn.

get along

He gets along with his in-laws.
No one can get along on those wages.

get around

It is hard to get around without a car.
Word got around somehow, even though it was supposed to be a secret.

get at

The cat hid where we couldn't get at it.
I don't know what you're getting at, so please explain yourself better.

get away

She wanted to come along but couldn't get away.

get back

Getting back to my main point, one should always strive to be honest.
We got back from Long Island last week.

get back at

There's no need to get back at them; ultimately, you will succeed.

get by

He just got by in high school, even though he is now a great success.
We'll get by if we save a little more.
His mistake got by the editor but was caught by the readers.

get down

Let's get down to work. There's much to do.
The heat was getting me down.
She got the pill down on the first try.

get in

We got in late last night.
I got in with the wrong crowd, and now I am paying for it.

get into

They got into trouble by stealing cars.
She got into gourmet cooking last year.

get off

He got the letter off in plenty of time.
He got off scot-free.
The attorney got her client off with a slap on the wrist.
He got off early and went fishing.

get on

She gets on well with the neighbors.
Get on with the performance!
I'm beginning to get on in age!
I have to get on the bus right away, so let me say good-bye now.

get out

We have to get out of here quickly.
Somehow the secret got out.
He got his most important book out last year.

get over

They finally got over the hard times.

get through

They got through very difficult times together.
How can I ever get through to you?

get to

The noise really gets to me.
I didn't get to the housework until Sunday.

get together

When should we get together?

get up

We get up early every day.
He got up a petition against rezoning.
I'm trying to get up the nerve to quit smoking.

get even

Getting even is never the best strategy. It's best to forget and let go.

get going

It's time to get going. We're late.

get nowhere

You will get nowhere with that idea.

get wind of

I got wind of the scheme only yesterday.

Exercise Set 10-4

A. Complete each phrase with the appropriate preposition.

1. getting _____ with people
2. getting _____ without a car
3. getting a point _____
4. getting _____ someone to do something
5. getting _____ some point
6. getting _____ for relaxation
7. getting _____ from vacation
8. getting _____ with little money
9. getting _____ to work
10. getting _____ late
11. getting _____ with the wrong crowd
12. getting _____ trouble
13. getting _____ with a slap on the wrist
14. getting _____ early

15. getting _____ well with people
16. getting _____ in age
17. getting _____ a new book
18. getting _____ hard times

B.   Match the parts in the two columns to make complete sentences.

1. It's late and thus it's time to
2. We got wind
3. You will get nowhere
4. Getting even is not always
5. Do you want to get
6. At what time do you
7. I've got to get up
8. The pollution in this city is
9. I've got to get
10. We sure got through

(a) a very difficult period of time.
(b) to work right away.
(c) getting to me.
(d) the nerve to do it.
(e) get up in the morning?
(f) the best way to resolve issues.
(g) together this weekend?
(h) with that kind of behavior.
(i) of the plot only now.
(j) get going.

Basic Vocabulary

*One forgets words as one forgets names. One's vocabulary
needs constant fertilizing or it will die.*

Evelyn Waugh (1903–1966)

Numbers and Measurement

1. It is impossible in a handbook to give a complete treatment of all the basic words you will need to become proficient in English. It all depends on what your specific needs and expectations are.

2. The objective of this chapter is to provide you with a list of basic vocabulary items that may be difficult to find organized in a "thematic" way in reference works such as dictionaries and glossaries.

3. One such theme is *numbers*—an area of vocabulary that is always problematic when learning another language. There are two types of numbers: *cardinal* numbers are used for counting (*one, two, three*, and so on); *ordinal numbers* are used to indicate order (*first, second, third*, and so on):

4. The cardinal numbers from 1 to 19 are:

1	*one*	11	*eleven*
2	*two*	12	*twelve*
3	*three*	13	*thirteen*
4	*four*	14	*fourteen*
5	*five*	15	*fifteen*
6	*six*	16	*sixteen*
7	*seven*	17	*seventeen*
8	*eight*	18	*eighteen*
9	*nine*	19	*nineteen*
10	*ten*		

5. The numbers from 20 onward are formed by attaching the words for the first nine numbers to each category of tens with a hyphen:

21	*twenty-one*
35	*thirty-five*
94	*ninety-four*
98	*ninety-eight*

6. Here are the relevant number words you will need:

20	*twenty*	60	*sixty*
30	*thirty*	70	*seventy*
40	*forty*	80	*eighty*
50	*fifty*	90	*ninety*

7. From 100 on, simply use *and* as shown:

| 234 | *two hundred and thirty-four* |
| 6,456 | *six thousand four hundred and fifty-six* |

8. Here are the main number words from 100 on:

100	*one hundred / a hundred*
1,000	*one thousand / a thousand*
1,000,000	*one million / a million*

9. Cardinal numbers are placed before nouns:

three people
fifty-eight minutes

10. The ordinal number words from 1 to 19 are as follows:

1st	*first*	11th	*eleventh*
2nd	*second*	12th	*twelfth*
3rd	*third*	13th	*thirteenth*
4th	*fourth*	14th	*fourteenth*
5th	*fifth*	15th	*fifteenth*
6th	*sixth*	16th	*sixteenth*
7th	*seventh*	17th	*seventeenth*
8th	*eighth*	18th	*eighteenth*
9th	*ninth*	19th	*nineteenth*
10th	*tenth*		

11. The number words for the remaining ordinals are easily constructed by attaching the first nine ordinals to the corresponding cardinal category with a hyphen:

21st	*twenty-first*
35th	*thirty-fifth*
94th	*ninety-fourth*
98th	*ninety-eighth*

12. The number words for the tens categories of ordinals themselves are formed by changing the *-y* ending to *-ieth*:

20th	*twentieth*
30th	*thirtieth*

13. For the other ordinals use *and* as shown below:

234th	*two hundred and thirty-fourth*
6,456th	*six thousand four hundred and fifty-sixth*

14. Ordinal numbers are adjectives that precede nouns:

the first day
the twentieth time
the ninety-fourth chapter
the ninety-eighth piece

15. Ordinals can be transformed into pronouns (see Chapter 5).

He is the third in line.

16. Ordinals are used to express the denominator of fractions, and cardinals, the numerator. If the numerator is greater than 1, the suffix *-s* (put at the end of the ordinal) must be used to show plurality:

1/5	*one-fifth*
1/8	*one-eighth*
3/4	*three-fourths*
9/10	*nine-tenths*
12/24	*twelve-twenty-fourths*

17. Notice the following exceptions:

1/2	*half / one-half / a half*
1/4	*one-fourth / one-quarter / a quarter*

18. A basic use of numbers is, of course, to indicate age:

    How old are you?   *I am twenty-eight years old.*
    How old is she?   *She must be around thirty.*

19. Note the following useful quantity expressions:

    double   *twice / two times*
    triple   *three times*
    a dozen   *twelve*
    about twenty   *approximately twenty*
    around thirty   *approximately thirty*

20. Compare the following two systems of measurement:

	U.S. Customary	Metric
Distance	1 inch	2.54 centimeters
	1 foot (12 inches)	0.3048 meter
	1 yard (3 feet)	0.91 meter
	1 mile (5,280 feet)	1.61 kilometers
	1 acre (43,560 square feet)	0.40 hectare
Weight	1 ounce	28.35 grams
	1 pound (16 ounces)	0.45 kilogram
Liquid	1 pint	0.5505 liter
	1 quart (2 pints)	0.95 liter
	1 gallon (4 quarts)	3.79 liters

Exercise Set 11-1

A. Write out the following numbers as indicated in the example.

Example: 234
            two hundred and thirty-four

1. 102
2. 567
3. 1,234
4. 23,798
5. 100,000
6. 134th

    7. 7,890
    8. 1/7
    9. 3/5
  10. 1/2

B.   Give the equivalent of each.

      Example: twice
                 double

    1. I am nearly twenty-eight years of age.
    2. three times
    3. a dozen
    4. 2.54 centimeters
    5. 0.91 meter
    6. 1.61 kilometers
    7. 28.35 grams
    8. 0.45 kilogram
    9. 0.5505 liter
  10. 3.79 liters

Telling Time

1.   Telling time is another important area of vocabulary to master. To indicate the hours, simply use the cardinal numbers as shown. Notice the use of the expletive *it* as a subject in sentences referring to time (see Chapter 5).

    What time is it?

    1:00   *It's one (o'clock).*
    2:00   *It's two (o'clock).*

2.   Morning, afternoon, and evening hours are indicated with the following expressions:

    10:00 A.M.   *Ten in the morning*
    2:00 P.M.   *Two in the afternoon*
    6:00 P.M.   *Six in the evening*
    11:00 P.M.   *Eleven at night*

3. Officially, time is based on the twenty-four-hour system. This is used, however, primarily by scientists, the military, pilots, and other such people. After the noon hour, official hours are indicated as follows:

| 1:00 P.M. | 1300 | or | *thirteen hundred hours* |
| 2:00 P.M. | 1400 | or | *fourteen hundred hours* |

4. Minutes are simply added to the hour as shown:

3:20	*It's three twenty.*
4:10	*It's four ten.*
9:53	*It's nine fifty-three.*

5. An alternative way is to use *past* or *after*:

| 3:20 | *It's twenty past three. / It's twenty after three.* |
| 4:10 | *It's ten past four. / It's ten after four.* |

6. As the next hour approaches, you can alternatively use *to* followed by the number of minutes remaining:

| 9:53 | *It's seven (minutes) to ten.* |
| 10:59 | *It's a minute to eleven.* |

7. The expression *quarter* can be used to refer to the quarter hours as shown:

| 10:15 | *It's ten fifteen. / It's a quarter past ten.* |
| 3:45 | *It's three forty-five. / It's a quarter to four.* |

8. The expression *half past* can be used to refer to the half hours as shown:

| 10:30 | *It's half past ten.* |
| 3:30 | *It's half past three.* |

9. Note the following useful words and expressions:

today	this day
morning	A.M. (before noon)
noon / midday	12 P.M.
afternoon	P.M. (until about 6 P.M.)
evening	P.M. (starting at about 6 P.M.)
tonight	this night
midnight	12 A.M.
tomorrow	the day after today

ago　gone by, in the past

He arrived twenty minutes ago.

in　to indicate a future action

He will arrive in twenty minutes.

watch	timepiece worn on the wrist or carried on the body
clock	timepiece not carried on body
dial	face of a watch or clock
The watch is fast.	somewhat ahead of the actual time
The watch is slow.	behind the correct time

exactly

It's exactly one o'clock.
It's three-thirty exactly.

or

on the dot

It's one o'clock on the dot.
It's three-thirty on the dot.

Exercise Set 11-2

A.　Write out the indicated times as shown in the example.

> *Example:*　2:15 A.M.
> *It's two fifteen in the morning. / It's a quarter past / after two in the morning.*

1. 6:10 A.M.
2. 7:30 P.M.
3. 12:00 A.M.
4. 12:00 P.M.
5. 1:55 P.M.
6. 9:15 A.M.

B.   Give an equivalent for each of the following.

Example: this day
              today

1. A.M. before noon
2. 12 P.M.
3. this night
4. the day after today
5. twenty minutes gone by
6. timepiece worn on the wrist
7. My watch shows a time that is behind the correct time.
8. face of a clock
9. It's exactly three o'clock.

Dates

1. Knowing how to express the date correctly is yet another important vocabulary skill.

   What is today's date?
   What day is it?
   It's September twenty-first.
   We arrived in the United States in January.
   My birthday is Monday, September the fifteenth.

2. The main vocabulary items you will require to talk about dates are the days of the week and the months of the year, which are listed here for your convenience:

Days of the week (in order)

Sunday
Monday
Tuesday
Wednesday
Thursday
Friday
Saturday

Months of the year (in order)

January
February
March
April
May
June
July
August
September
October
November
December

3. The expression for indicating recurring actions or activities on a specific day of the week is

on Mondays	*On Mondays I always go for a swim.*
on Tuesdays	*On Tuesdays we have music lessons.*

4. The preposition *in* is used instead with the singular form of the month:

Every February we often go to the sea.   or   *In February we go to the sea.*
Each May there is a lot of sunshine.   or   *In May there is a lot of sunshine.*

5. Notice that the days and months are always capitalized, no matter where they occur in a sentence.

6. The seasons may or may not be capitalized (unless they occur as the first word in a sentence):

spring
summer
fall
winter

7. Note the following useful expressions:

next (after that)

He is coming to visit next month.

last (previous)

They were here last Tuesday.

until / till (awaiting, up to)

They are staying till August.

a ... from (since, time duration)

A week from tomorrow is Easter.

8. Dates are expressed as shown below:

Today is January 29 (the twenty-ninth or twenty-nine).
Today is September 15 (the fifteenth or fifteen).
Today is Monday, March 16 (the sixteenth or sixteen).
Today is Wednesday, December 4 (the fourth or four).

Exercise Set 11-3

A. Indicate the appropriate day of the week, month of the year, or season.

1. the day after Saturday
2. the day before Friday
3. the second day after Monday
4. the day before Wednesday
5. the first and last months of the year
6. the month in which Valentine's Day is celebrated
7. the month after March
8. the month before June
9. the month in which Independence Day is celebrated
10. the month after August
11. the month in which Halloween is celebrated
12. the month in which Thanksgiving is celebrated
13. the season of hot weather
14. the season of cold weather
15. the season when the leaves fall
16. the season after winter

B.   Give the equivalent.

   Example: every Monday
   	 on Mondays

   1. every Saturday
   2. every September
   3. after that
   4. up to
   5. September 21
   6. April 4

The Weather and Directions

   1.   Knowing how to talk about the weather is another basic skill. Again, notice the use of *it* as an expletive when talking about the weather (see Chapter 5).

   How's the weather?
   What's the weather like?
   What's the temperature outside?

   It's beautiful.
   It's awful.
   It's hot.
   It's cloudy.
   It's cold.
   It's very hot.
   It's freezing.
   It's rather cool outside.
   It's raining.
   It's snowing.
   It's sunny.
   It's thundering.
   It's warm.
   It's windy.

2. Here are some useful words and expressions related to time and to the weather:

dawn	the time each morning at which daylight first begins
twilight	the time of day when the sun is just below the horizon
dusk	darker stage of twilight
sunrise	appearance of the sun above the eastern horizon
sunset	disappearance of the sun below the western horizon
storm	atmospheric disturbance manifested by strong winds accompanied by rain, snow, or other precipitation and often by thunder and lightning
hurricane	severe tropical cyclone
blizzard	very heavy snowstorm with high winds
tornado	violent windstorm accompanied by a funnel-shaped downward extension of cloud
clap of thunder	sound made by thunder
bolt of lightning	flash of lightning

3. Here are the words for the main directions:

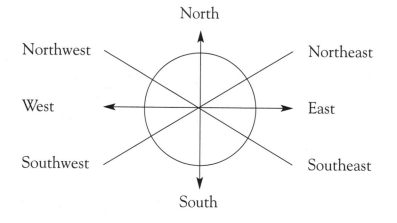

Exercise Set 11-4

A. Give a synonym for each word or expression.

   Example: flash of lightning
                  bolt of lightning

   1. sound made by thunder
   2. heavy snowstorm
   3. tropical cyclone
   4. It's very, very cold.
   5. It's hot (but not too hot).

B. Now, give the opposite of each word or expression.

   Example: It's cold.
                  It's hot.

   1. north
   2. east
   3. southeast
   4. northeast
   5. sunrise
   6. dawn
   7. It's cloudy.
   8. It's awful.
   9. It's cold.

Synonyms and Antonyms

1. *Synonyms* are words that have the same or approximately the same meaning. *Antonyms* are words that have an opposite meaning. Being able to identify words as synonyms or antonyms will help you learn and remember vocabulary.

2. Keep in mind that no two words have exactly the same meaning in every situation.

Word / expression	Synonyms
ask	inquire
crazy	insane, mad
face	countenance
gladly	willingly, happily
much	a lot
near	close, next to
nothing	zero
now	at present
only	merely, just
(to) please	(to) satisfy
quick	fast
same	identical
slowly	bit by bit
street	road
suit	outfit
therefore	thus
truly	really
(to) understand	(to) know

3. Keep in mind, again, that no two words have exactly the opposite meaning in every situation:

Word / expression	Antonyms
sunrise	sunset
beautiful	ugly
clean	dirty
clear	dark
(to) come	(to) go
early	late
easy	difficult
empty	full
entrance	exit
everything	nothing
(to) find	(to) lose
first	last

good	*bad*
inside	*outside*
landing	*take-off*
much, a lot	*little, a bit*
near	*far*
nice, pleasant	*unpleasant*
often	*never*
old	*young*
open	*closed*
rich	*poor*
(to) sell	*(to) buy*
small	*big*
tall	*short*
thin, skinny	*fat*
well	*bad, poorly*
white	*black*
(to) borrow	*(to) lend*

Exercise Set 11-5

A.   Give a synonym for each word.

1. crazy
2. gladly
3. much
4. nothing
5. quick
6. same
7. street
8. therefore
9. truly
10. understand

B.   Give an antonym for each word.

1. beautiful
2. clean
3. clear
4. easy

5. empty
6. entrance
7. good
8. inside
9. near
10. open
11. rich
12. tall

Suffixes and Commonly Confused Words

1. Another effective way to learn and remember vocabulary is to recognize the meanings and functions of suffixes. For example, if a noun ends in *-or* or *-er*, it often refers to a person involved in some kind of job or profession:

    actor
    doctor
    professor
    lawyer
    baker

2. If a noun ends in *-logy* or *-ics*, it normally refers to an area of study (a subject, a discipline, and so on):

    biology
    anthropology
    zoology
    psychology
    mathematics
    ethics
    bionics

3. If a noun ends in *–ist*, it typically refers to a person who is involved in a profession or who possesses some particular knowledge or skill:

    dentist
    biologist
    cellist
    pianist
    artist

4. Other endings can be found in Chapter 4.

5. Finally, here are pairs of words that are commonly confused by ESL learners. Be careful!

accept	to take something offered	*I accept your offer.*
except	other than	*Everyone went to the party except her.*
advice	opinion given	*His sister gave him the correct advice.*
advise	to counsel	*His sister advised him to study medicine.*
affect	to influence	*Her decision did not affect me.*
effect	to cause to happen	*The medicine took effect right away.*
emigrate	to leave a country	*They emigrated from Japan to the United States.*
immigrate	to come into a country	*They immigrated to the United States last year.*
its	possessive of *it*	*Our city must improve its roads.*
it's	contraction of *it is*	*It's your duty to help them out.*
principal	head of a high school	*She's the principal of our school.*
principle	a belief, code, or rule	*The principles of quantum physics are difficult.*
than	conjunction	*He is older than I am.*
then	adverb	*We lived in New York; then we moved to Chicago.*
their	possessive of *they*	*That is their house.*
they're	contraction of *they are*	*They're leaving for Vermont next week.*

there	adverb (at that place)	*I put it over there.*
	expletive	*There are many people in this class.*
your	possessive of *you*	*Is this your book?*
you're	contraction of *you are*	*I know you're going to succeed in life.*

Exercise Set 11-6

A. Check (✔) the category to which each noun belongs.

	Job / profession	*Subject / discipline*
violinist		
anthropology		
carpenter		
ethics		
electronics		
singer		
tailor		

B. Choose (a) or (b) correctly.

1. Everyone goes on vacation _____ me.
   (a) accept
   (b) except

2. Your decision does not _____ us in any way.
   (a) affect
   (b) effect

3. They _____ to the United States recently.
   (a) emigrated
   (b) immigrated

4. Our legal system must simply improve _____ administrative procedures.
   (a) its
   (b) it's

5. The _____ of analytic geometry are not hard to understand.
   (a) principles
   (b) principals

6. I am _____ friend.
   (a) their
   (b) they're

7. Is this _____ idea?
   (a) your
   (b) you're

— 12 —

Basic Conversation

Ideal conversation must be an exchange of thought, and not,
as many of those who worry most about their shortcomings
believe, an eloquent exhibition of wit or oratory.

Emily Post (1873–1960)

What Is a Conversation?

1. A *conversation* is a spoken exchange of thoughts, opinions, and feelings. Knowing how to converse involves knowing which words, phrases, expressions, and types of sentences apply to a given situation.

What's your name?	*My name is Miguel Carrera.*
How old are you?	*I am twenty-eight years old.*
Where do you live?	*I live near Chicago.*
How are you?	*Not bad, and you?*
Thank-you.	*You're welcome.*

2. By mastering the grammar covered by this book, you already know quite a bit about conversing. For instance, you know which interrogative words to use when asking questions, which imperative verb forms are needed to give commands, and so on.

3. However, there are some aspects of communication that are purely formulaic. The objective of this very brief chapter is to provide you with a few common expressions that occur frequently in conversations. If you know them already, this is your chance to brush up on them.

Exercise Set 12-1

A. Provide an appropriate word to complete each sentence.

1. I live _____ New York.
2. I am thirty years _____ .
3. My _____ is Gina Carletti.
4. I do not _____ what you just said.
5. Can you _____ more slowly?

B. Now, formulate an appropriate question according to the given response.

Example: I am twenty-nine years old.
   How old are you?

1. I am quite well, thanks.
2. I live in Houston.
3. My name is Maria Pereira.
4. It's ten thirty.
5. It's September 15.
6. It's very cold.
7. He's sixty-five years old.

Starting and Ending Conversations

1. To greet someone politely (strangers, superiors, and so on), use expressions such as the following ones according to the time of day:

Hello / Good morning Mr. Gauthier. How's it going?
Well, thanks, and you?

Hello / Good afternoon, Mrs. Carrera. How are you?
Not bad, thanks.

Hello / Good evening, Mrs. Rossi. How are you?
Quite well, thanks, and you?

2. To greet someone informally (friends, family members, and the like), use the following:

    Hi, how's it going?
    Very well, and you?

    Greetings, how are you?
    So, so.

    Hey there, what's up?
    Not much. What about you?

3. Notice the relevant expressions that apply to telephone greetings:

    Hello.
    Who's speaking? / Who is it? / Who is this?
    With whom am I speaking?
    This is Dino Franceschi.
    Is Mr. Smith there?

4. The following can be used to end conversations and to take leave of someone:

    Have a good day!
    Have a good evening!
    Good-bye!

    Informal:

    Bye!
    See you soon!
    See you!
    See you later!
    Take care!
    So long!

Exercise Set 12-2

A. Choose the appropriate response, (a) or (b).

1. How are you?
   (a) Quite well, thanks, and you?
   (b) Take care!

2. How's it going?
   (a) Good morning.
   (b) Well, thanks, and you?

3. Good evening, how are you?
   (a) See you later.
   (b) Not bad, thanks.

4. Hey there, what's up?
   (a) Not much. What about you?
   (b) Bye.

5. Who is it?
   (a) This is Jack Brown.
   (b) Is Jack Brown there?

B. Complete the following pieces of conversation by adding the missing parts.

1. With _____ am I speaking?
2. Have a _____ day!
3. See you _____ !
4. So _____ !
5. Take _____ !
6. Who is _____ ?

Other Common Expressions

1. Here are a few expressions that you can use for introducing people:

    Let me introduce you to Mary.
    Allow me to introduce you to Mrs. Gentile.
    Let me introduce you to Alexander Gauthier.

    A pleasure to make your acquaintance.
    Glad to meet you.
    Delighted to meet you.

2. Polite expressions will also come in handy in everyday conversation. Here are the most frequently used ones:

    Excuse me.
    Thanks a lot.
    Thanks a million!
    Sorry!
    My apologies!
    No matter!

3. Finally, here are some expressions that allow you to express basic emotions:

    Surprise

    Really?
    How come?
    Are you kidding?
    Unbelievable! / Incredible!

    Agreement / disagreement

    Good idea!
    OK.
    I agree.
    I'm fine with that.

It's not OK.
I don't agree.
I disagree.
No way! (can also indicate surprise or disbelief)
Impossible!

Pity / resignation

Too bad. / It's a pity.
I'm sorry.
How sad!
There's nothing to do.
Patience!

Indifference / boredom

It doesn't matter.
It's all the same to me.
Ugh!
Enough!
What a bore!

Exercise Set 12-3

A. Provide the missing words.

1. Excuse _____ .
2. Thanks a _____ !
3. Glad to _____ you.
4. A pleasure to make your _____ .
5. Allow me to _____ you to Julie Bergin.
6. _____ to meet you.

B.   Indicate what type of emotion each expression allows you to convey.

   Example: Ugh!
               boredom

   1. It doesn't matter.
   2. I'm sorry.
   3. No way!
   4. I'm fine with that.
   5. There's nothing to do.
   6. Really?
   7. Are you kidding?

— 13 —

Basic Modes of Expression

*Methinks the human method of expression by sound of tongue
is very elementary, and ought to be substituted for some
ingenious invention which should be able to give vent to
at least six coherent sentences at once.*

Virginia Woolf (1882–1941)

Expressing Likes, Dislikes, and Preferences

1. An *expression* is a word or group of words that communicates an idea, a feeling, an attitude, or another meaning. A *mode* of expression is a way of saying something that is generally peculiar to a given language. For example, languages have different modes to express likes, dislikes, and preferences. To do so in English, use the verbs *like*, *dislike*, and *prefer* as shown below:

    like
    I like baseball.
    I would like some coffee.
    How do you like his nerve!
    If she likes, we can meet her there.

    dislike
    I dislike baseball.

    prefer
    He prefers juice to milk.

2. *Like* and *dislike* can also be used as nouns:
    He made a list of his likes and dislikes.

3. The negative form of *like*—*I do not like baseball*—is not as strong as *disklike*—*I dislike baseball*—which adds the idea of distaste or aversion to the meaning.

4. Note the following synonymous expressions:

What would you prefer to do?	*What would you rather do?*
I really like gardening.	*I am quite fond of gardening.*
I really like traveling.	*I am really fond of traveling.*
I really like my grandmother.	*I love my grandmother.*
I really dislike football.	*I hate football.*
I do not really like seafood.	*I do not care for seafood.*

5. Verbs such as *love, enjoy, relish, fancy,* and *dote on* are often used as synonyms for *like*, with these differences:

like
the least forceful, suggests mere interest, approval, or favor:

I like him, not love him!

love
implies a strong attachment or intense affection on an emotional level:

I love him, even though I do not like him!

enjoy
conveys satisfaction or pleasure:

First, you should get what you like, and after that, enjoy it.

relish
conveys greater satisfaction or pleasure:

I relish eating pizza; it's my favorite food.

fancy
refers to something that appeals to one's taste or imagination:

My sister fancies only trendy clothes.

dote on
implies foolish, extravagant attachment:

He dotes on his grandchildren and indulges their every whim.

6. To convey intense dislike use *hate*:

   I really hate baseball, not just dislike it.

7. In some languages, such as Spanish and Italian, the verb *like* corresponds to verbs that mean "to be pleasing to." If you speak such a language, be careful! *I like baseball* would be equivalent to *Baseball is pleasing to me.*

Exercise Set 13-1

A. Fill in the blanks with *like, enjoy, dote, relish, dislike,* or *prefer,* according to sense.

1. I really _____ driving in rush hour traffic. It drives me insane!
2. I _____ walking to driving.
3. If you _____ baseball so much, why do you keep on watching it on TV?
4. I would _____ some sugar with my coffee, please.
5. I do not _____ tea; I _____ coffee.
6. You should _____ your good life.
7. I _____ pasta more than anything else.
8. She _____ her children.

B. Give a synonymous expression.

1. I really like playing the piano.
2. I really like my friend.
3. I really dislike that song.
4. I fancy good clothes.
5. She dislikes going out.

Miscellaneous Expressions

1. To express your opinions, verbs and expressions such as *be right / wrong, be sure / not sure, think, in my view,* and the like will come in handy:

   to be (in)correct, (in)appropriate:

   You're right to resign. / You're wrong to resign.

   to hold a belief:

   Personally, I believe that he doesn't mean it. / I think you are mistaken.

   to have a feeling about:

   I feel that we ought to be more active.

   to hold a conviction:

   I'm convinced that she's responsible.

   to have a point of view:

   In my view, you should go ahead and do it. / To my mind, you are right.

2. To convey degrees of uncertainty use the modal verb *may, might, must,* or *could* as shown:

Certainty	Small degree of uncertainty	Greater degree of uncertainty
He is Italian.	*He must be Italian.*	*He may / might/ could be Italian.*
She loves him.	*She must love him.*	*She may / might / could love him.*

3. Modal verbs can also be used to convey politeness:

   May I use your phone, please?
   Could I borrow your pen for a second?
   Can I use your phone, please?
   Would you mind letting me use your phone?
   Could you tell me where Main Street is?
   Can you please tell me where the bathroom is?

4. Notice that *Would you mind?* must be followed by the gerund if making a request. If asking permission it must be followed by *if + subject + verb*:

   Would you mind closing the door?
   Would you mind if we left early?

5. The modal verbs *must* and *have to* allow you to express necessity:

   Everyone must take that exam before graduating.
   Do I also have to take the exam?

6. When used in the negative, the meaning of these modal verbs changes:

   must not / mustn't (prohibition)
   You must not eat so much meat!

   do not / don't have to (lack of necessity)
   You do not have to take the exam.

7. *Should, had better,* and *ought to* allow you to express the same kinds of meanings:

   You should study harder for that exam.
   You had better study harder for that exam.
   You shouldn't study so hard.
   You ought to eat less than you do.
   You had better not be late for the exam.

8. *Be supposed to* allows you to express the notion that someone expects something to occur. In the past it indicates that the expected action didn't occur:

   The game is supposed to begin in an hour.
   Weren't you supposed to call me last night?

9. To make suggestions, you have several choices:

   let's (let us) followed by the simple form of the infinitive (without to):

   Let's go to the movies tonight, OK?
   Let's not stay home, no matter what.

   Why do + not + simple infinitive (friendly suggestion):

   Why don't we go to the movies tonight?
   Why don't you both just stop quarreling?

   shall (suggestion implying agreement):

   Shall we go to the movies tonight? Is that OK with you?
   Shall I call you tomorrow?

   could (an indirect suggestion):

   Where should we go tonight? We could go to the movies.

10. Below are expressions for giving advice:

    should (definite advice) / should have (hindsight advice):

    I'm having trouble with grammar. You should read more.
    I failed my math test. You should have studied more.

    could (suggestions or possibilities) / could have (hindsight possibilities):

    I'm having trouble with grammar. You could try reading more or taking a course.
    I failed my math test. You could have studied more or I could have tried to help you.

Exercise Set 13-2

A. Match the parts in the two columns to make complete sentences.

1. You had better not be late	(a) drink only soda pop.
2. You must not	(b) for your own wedding.
3. You have to	(c) speaking more loudly?
4. Would you mind	(d) take that exam over.
5. May I	(e) be her boyfriend, don't you
6. He must	think?
7. I'm convinced that he	(f) is right.
8. You're right	(g) use your phone?
9. I feel that	(h) you should do that.
	(i) to think that.

B. Fill in the blanks with *be supposed to, let's, shall, should, could, should have,* or *could have,* as the case may be.

1. _____ go out right now, OK?
2. The game _____ begin soon.
3. _____ I call you tonight to set something up?
4. Where _____ we go? We _____ go to the park.
5. I know I _____ study more in order to become proficient in English.
6. I failed that test. I _____ studied more.
7. If you're having trouble with grammar, you _____ try taking a course.

Expressions with *Be* and *Take*

1. Many expressions are constructed with the verb *be.* You have encountered quite a number of them in illustrative sentences throughout this book:

be about to

He is about to enter high school.

> **The Verb *Be***
>
> Simple present:
>
> *(I) am, (you) are, (he / she / it) is, (we) are, (they) are*
>
> Simple past:
>
> *(I) was, (you) were, (he / she / it) was, (we) were, (they) were*
>
> Present participle:
>
> *being*
>
> Past participle:
>
> *been*

be quiet

You must be quiet when you are in a library.

be up to someone

It's up to her to get that task finished.

2. There are also many useful expressions constructed with the verb *take*. Here are a few of them. You may have to look them up in a dictionary.

take after

He takes after his grandfather.

take apart

She took my argument apart.

take back

I take it all back. I was wrong.

take for

Do you take me for a fool?

take in

I couldn't take in the meaning of the word.
She was taken in by a con artist.
We took in the sights.

take off

Take your jacket off. It's warm in here.
The plane took off on time.
I'm taking off three days during February.
Her invention has taken off and is now sold all over the country.

take on

I took on too many extra responsibilities.
Over the years he has taken on the look of a banker.

take out

Don't take out your frustration in such an aggressive manner.
I took out the money owed in services.

take over

He took over as CEO of the company.

take up

Let's take up where we left off.
Let's take up each problem one at a time.

take account of

You must always take your family's interest into account.

take care

Take care or you will slip on the ice.

take charge

I must take charge of my own life.

take effect

The antibiotics at last began to take effect.

take for granted

He took his family for granted.

take it

If you can dish it out, you've got to learn to take it.

take (one's) time

There's no rush. Take all the time you need.

take place

All that took place while we were away.

take root

His ideas have finally taken root.

take shape

Those ideas took shape a long time ago.

take sides

Do not take sides in the argument!

take the floor

The senator took the floor yesterday.

Exercise Set 13-3

A. Match the parts in the columns to make complete sentences.

1. I am about
2. You should be
3. It's up to you
4. That girl takes
5. Why do you always take
6. I take
7. I do not take you

(a) after her mother.
(b) my arguments apart?
(c) it all back.
(d) for a fool.
(e) to finish it.
(f) quiet when others are
      studying.
(g) to go home.

B.   Fill in the blanks with the missing words.

1   We took _____ the sights of Chicago.
2. Did the plane take _____ on time?
3. You're taking _____ too much work.
4. I always take _____ my frustration by shouting at my dog.
5. Did she take _____ as director?
6. Take _____ of yourself.
7. The aspirins will start taking _____ soon.
8. One should never take loved ones for _____ .
9. Take all the _____ you need.
10. My ideas have finally taken _____ .
11. His ideas took _____ a long time ago.
12. You should never take _____ in arguments!

— 14 —

Written Communication

*I hold that the parentheses are by far the most
important parts of a non-business letter.*

D. H. Lawrence (1885–1930)

Correspondence

1. An important aspect of written communication is letter writing, whether traditional (mail-delivered) or electronic (e-mail). There are two main kinds of letters: *formal* (used when applying for a job, when writing to someone in authority, and so on) and *informal* (used when writing to friends, acquaintances, and so on).

2. The main parts of a formal letter are shown below:

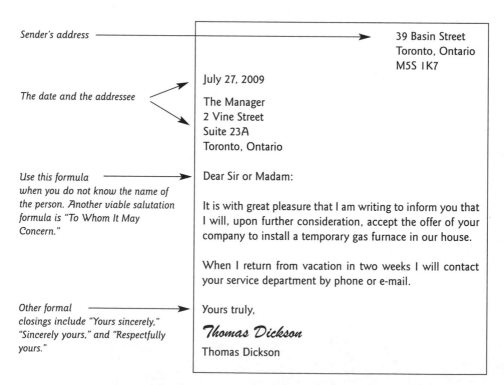

Sender's address → 39 Basin Street / Toronto, Ontario / M5S 1K7

The date and the addressee → July 27, 2009 / The Manager / 2 Vine Street / Suite 23A / Toronto, Ontario

Use this formula when you do not know the name of the person. Another viable salutation formula is "To Whom It May Concern." → Dear Sir or Madam:

It is with great pleasure that I am writing to inform you that I will, upon further consideration, accept the offer of your company to install a temporary gas furnace in our house.

When I return from vacation in two weeks I will contact your service department by phone or e-mail.

Other formal closings include "Yours sincerely," "Sincerely yours," and "Respectfully yours." → Yours truly,

Thomas Dickson

Thomas Dickson

3. The main parts of an informal letter are shown below:

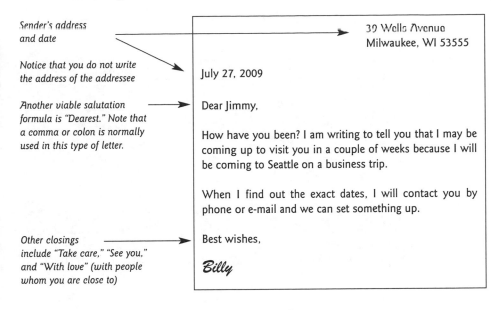

Sender's address and date

Notice that you do not write the address of the addressee

Another viable salutation formula is "Dearest." Note that a comma or colon is normally used in this type of letter.

Other closings include "Take care," "See you," and "With love" (with people whom you are close to)

> 39 Wells Avenue
> Milwaukee, WI 53555
>
> July 27, 2009
>
> Dear Jimmy,
>
> How have you been? I am writing to tell you that I may be coming up to visit you in a couple of weeks because I will be coming to Seattle on a business trip.
>
> When I find out the exact dates, I will contact you by phone or e-mail and we can set something up.
>
> Best wishes,
>
> *Billy*

4. Here are the parts of an envelope:

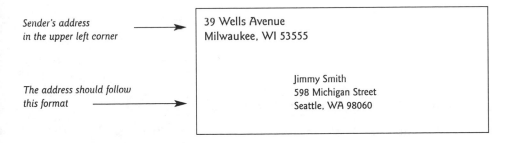

Sender's address in the upper left corner

The address should follow this format

> 39 Wells Avenue
> Milwaukee, WI 53555
>
>   Jimmy Smith
>   598 Michigan Street
>   Seattle, WA 98060

Exercise Set 14-1

A. Indicate (with a check mark ✔) if the salutation or closing belongs to a formal or an informal letter.

	Formal	Informal
To Whom It May Concern:		
Best wishes,		
Take care,		
Sincerely yours,		
Yours sincerely,		
With love,		
See you,		
Dear John,		
Dear Sir or Madam:		
Respectfully yours,		

B. The following parts of an envelope are out of order. Put them in order.

Chicago, Illinois 60614
Michigan Avenue, 42

Doolittle Mary
Memphis, Tennessee 38163
Main Street, 34

Punctuation, Capitalization, and Spelling

1. *Punctuation* is the use of marks and signs in writing and printing to separate words into sentences, clauses, and phrases in order to clarify meaning. For example, there are three ways to end a sentence:

    With a period: *I ate all the soup.*
    With a question mark: *Who ate all the soup?*
    With an exclamation point: *Eat all the soup right away!*

2. A period indicates a full stop. It is placed at the end of affirmative sentences and other statements.

    She is my best friend.
    We went out, even though it was raining.

3. A period is often used after abbreviations and initials

Wednesday	*Wed.*
Doctor	*Dr.*
John F. Kenney	*J. F. K.*

4. A question mark is placed at the end of an interrogative sentence:

Is he coming as well?
He is coming too?

5. An exclamation point is placed at the end of an emphatic sentence:

Leave me alone!
You are going to win!

6. A comma is used to indicate a separation of ideas or of elements within the structure of a sentence.

It is used

when more than one modifier is employed to describe a noun:

Their house has a long, dark, narrow basement.

with introductory structures:

After working hard all day, he comes home rather tired.

before some types of clauses:

I thought he was coming, but I was mistaken.

if a phrase follows, do not use a comma:

I knew he was coming but leaving early.

after interjections and before tags:

Oh, I'm so glad to see you.
You're coming too, aren't you?

before and after transitional or parenthetical forms:

You'll find, therefore, that I am right.
He is, I believe, rather old.

with direct quotations:

"Please call me," he said.
"I'm not sure what to do," he added, "if you do not come."

in dates with the month, day, and year:

October 23, 1958

after *yes* and *no* in responses:

"Yes, I'm coming too."
"No, he's not coming."

7. A semicolon is used to connect independent clauses so as to indicate a closer relationship between the clauses than a period does:

   Reading is important; watching TV is not.

8. A semicolon is also used before a conjunctive structure such as *then, however, hence, that is, in fact, still, thus,* and so on:

   I would like to come too; however, I will be working at that time.

9. A colon is used after a word introducing a quotation, an explanation, an example, or a series, with subtitles, and often after the salutation in a business letter:

   He had only one goal in life: to play baseball.
   She said: "I am coming too."
   Dear Madam or Sir:
   Please send the following: two erasers, five pencils, and six cards.
   Lucy: Growing Up Human

10. A dash is used to indicate a break or an interpolation in a sentence, or to summarize:

The boy who came yesterday—as we all know—is his grandson.
Fruits and vegetables—these are the staples of good health.

11. Parentheses are used to set off ideas that are only loosely connected to the meaning of the sentence:

Most people (at least, the ones I know) liked that movie.

12. Quotation marks are used to set off quoted words, phrases, and sentences:

"I will come too," said Alice.
The word "naïve" is derived from the French.

13. The apostrophe is used

to form contractions:

I cannot	*I can't*
I will	*I'll*
it is	*it's*

to indicate the plural form of letters and figures:

p's and q's	*0's and 1's*

to indicate possession:

singular:

of the neighbor	*the neighbor's*

plural:

of the teachers	*the teachers'*

14. Hyphens are used for many reasons. In general, hyphenate two or more words when they are used as adjectives preceding a noun:

    a well-known person
    a twelve-foot ceiling
    up-to-date information
    on-the-job training

15. Ellipsis points are three dots used to show that something has been omitted:

    I pledge allegiance to the flag ....

16. In general, capitalize the first word in a sentence, all proper nouns, the first word in a direct quotation, and the most important words in titles of books, movies, and so on.

    Proper nouns:

Names:	*Alex, Sarah*
Surnames:	*Ms. Jones, Dr. Smith*
Spacecraft, aircraft:	*Apollo 12, Boeing 727*
Deities:	*God, Buddha*
Periods:	*Ice Age, World War II*
Astronomical bodies:	*Venus, Milky Way*
Organizations:	*Yankees, Kiwanis Club*
Places:	*America, Milwaukee, the South*
Government bodies:	*Parliament, House of Commons*

    Titles:

    Of Mice and Men
    Sonata in D-Minor
    The Matrix

17. A *contraction* is a word, such as *won't* (*will not*), or phrase, such as *o'clock* (*of the clock*), formed by omitting or combining some of the parts of a longer phrase. The contraction is shown by an apostrophe ('). Contractions generally belong to informal speech.

18. Certain forms of *be* and *have* used as auxiliaries in compound tenses, and question words are usually contracted (in informal speech):

Verb and contraction	With a pronoun	With an interrogative (This is how it is said, but not necessarily written.)
am = *'m*	*I'm reading right now.*	—
is = *'s*	*He's outside playing.* *She's inside studying.* *It's raining.*	*Where's Mary?* *How's it going?* *Who's there?*
are = *'re*	*You're working too hard.* *They're not coming.*	*How're you doing?* *What're you saying?*
has = *'s*	*He's been here a while.* *She's seen it already.* *It's been hot lately.*	*Where's she been living?* *What's he said?*
have = *'ve*	*We've been there.* *They've done that already.*	*Where've you been?* *How've you accomplished that?*
had = *'d*	*He'd been there a while.* *They'd done that already.*	*Where'd you been when I called?* *How'd they survive all that?*
did = *'d*	—	*How'd you do on the exam?* *What'd you do last night?*
will = *'ll*	*He'll come if he can.* *She'll help you.*	*Who'll come to the party?* *Where'll you be tonight?*
would = *'d*	*He'd like to come as well.* *She'd come if she could.*	*Where'd you like to go?*

19. Auxiliary verbs also contract commonly with *not* (*'nt*):

   Aren't you coming as well?
   Don't you believe her?
   He won't go alone.
   They can't come either.

20. Finally, here is a list of commonly misspelled words:

   accommodate
   achieve
   acquire
   believe
   benefited
   embarrass
   existence
   February

height
occurring
perceive
precede
proceed
pursue
receive
similar

Exercise Set 14-2

A.   Missing from each sentence is the appropriate punctuation or capitalization. Provide it.

   1. we went out even though it was rather cold
   2. is he coming as well
   3. give me that pen right away
   4. their apartment has long narrow and dark corridors
   5. when he arrived we decided to go out
   6. ah why did you do that
   7. shes here isnt she
   8. please stay on the line she said
   9. staying calm is important shouting is not
   10. she asked whats your name

B.   Each of the following words is misspelled. Correct each one.

   1. acomodate
   2. accquire
   3. beleive
   4. benefitted
   5. embarass
   6. existance
   7. procede
   8. persue
   9. recieve

10. similer
11. Febuary
12. heihgt
13. ocuring
14. percieve
15. preceed
16. acheive

Online Communication

1. Today, written communication is taking place more and more through e-mails and other electronic forms. Here are words and expressions related to basic online concepts:

attachment	a document or file attached to an e-mail message
bookmark	an electronic marker inserted in a word processor document for later use
browser	computer software that allows an Internet user to search on the Web
chat room	an Internet location where participants exchange comments in real time
click on	a single action of pressing and releasing a button on a computer mouse
command	an instruction to a computer to carry out an operation
cut and paste	removing data from one place and inserting it somewhere else
cyberspace	the "space" in which electronic communication occurs
dot	a punctuation mark used to separate the components of an Internet address
download	copying data from one computer or Web site to another computer

e-commerce	business conducted through the Internet
e-mail	an electronic letter sent through the Internet
FAQs	frequently asked questions
icon	a small image on a computer screen that represents something visually
Internet	a network linking computers by satellite and telephone
ISP	Internet service provider: a business that provides access to the Internet
newsgroup	a discussion group on the Internet where users leave messages for others to read
online	attached to the Internet through a central computer
password	a sequence of characters needed to gain access to a computer system
search engine	a computer program that searches for keywords throughout the Internet and returns a list of documents in which they were found
server	a computer in a network that stores programs and data files accessed by other computers in the network
snail mail	mail sent through the postal service, as distinct from the faster e-mail
spam	unsolicited messages received through the Internet
surf the Net	to go on the Internet and shift from site to site
Web	(World Wide Web) the set of linked documents located on computers through the Internet
Web site (site)	a group of related Web pages

2. Online communication has also generated a new collection of common abbreviations and symbols that help enhance the speed of written communication. Here are some common ones, most of which are nothing more than made up of the first letters of the words they replace:

2	to
2day	today
2nite	tonight
2U	to you
4	for
afaik	as far as I know
b4	before
brb	be right back
btw	by the way
cid	consider it done
coz	because
cu	see you
ez	easy
fwiw	for what it's worth
fyi	for your information
gbtm	get back to me
gr8	great
gtg	got to go
hth	hope this helps
imo	in my opinion
iou	I owe you
l8r	later
msg	message
myob	mind your own business
ne1	anyone
no1	no one
np	no problem
nrn	no reply necessary
pls	please
rn	right now

ru	are you
ruok	are you ok
s/o	someone
s/th	something
thx	thanks
tmb	text me back
u	you
v	very
wan2	want to
wbs	write back soon
w/o	without
wud	what are you doing
y	why

3. E-mail messages are less formal than letters. Instead of the addresses shown previously, an e-mail has the following parts. Notice that the addresses of the sender and receiver consist of their e-mail addresses. In addition, the format contains a section *(Subject)* in which you can indicate the purpose of your message (in summary form) and a section indicating the date of the message and the time it was sent:

From:	marcel.danesi@utoronto.ca
To:	facultyofarts@utoronto.ca
Subject:	New course
Date:	April 4, ..., 10:52:32

I am writing to inquire about a new course I am supposed to teach. Can you inform me as to what time and in which classroom it will take place?

Thank you

MD

Exercise Set 14-3

A. Match the terms with their meanings.

    1. attachment   (a) business conducted online

    2. chat room   (b) a document or file attached to an e-mail

    3. click on   message

    4. spam   (c) an online location where participants

    5. snail mail   exchange comments

    6. icon   (d) pressing and releasing a button on a

    7. FAQs   computer mouse

    8. e-commerce   (e) unsolicited messages received through

        the Internet

        (f) mail sent through the postal service

        (g) image on a computer screen

        (h) frequently asked questions

B. Give an appropriate online abbreviation for each expression.

    1. today

    2. to you

    3. before

    4. by the way

    5. see you

    6. easy

    7. great

    8. got to go

    9. no reply necessary

    10. thanks

Résumés

1. A *résumé*, also called a *curriculum vitae*, is a brief written account of one's professional or work experience and qualifications, often submitted with an employment application. The general form and contents of an American résumé are shown below:

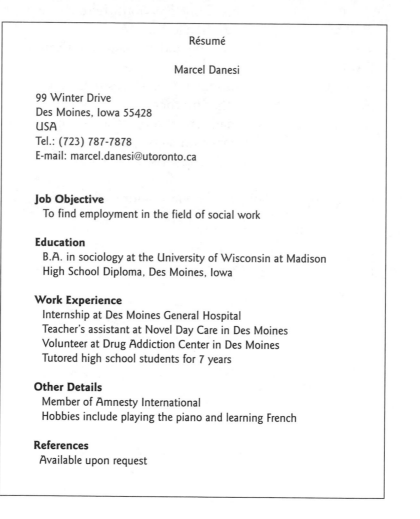

Résumé

Marcel Danesi

99 Winter Drive
Des Moines, Iowa 55428
USA
Tel.: (723) 787-7878
E-mail: marcel.danesi@utoronto.ca

Job Objective
  To find employment in the field of social work

Education
  B.A. in sociology at the University of Wisconsin at Madison
  High School Diploma, Des Moines, Iowa

Work Experience
  Internship at Des Moines General Hospital
  Teacher's assistant at Novel Day Care in Des Moines
  Volunteer at Drug Addiction Center in Des Moines
  Tutored high school students for 7 years

Other Details
  Member of Amnesty International
  Hobbies include playing the piano and learning French

References
  Available upon request

2. Notice that your name goes on the top followed by your address, phone, and e-mail information. These are followed by

Job Objective	why you are applying for a job
Work Experience	all the places where you have worked

Education	the schooling and training you have received (with relevant diplomas, degrees, and so on)
Other Details	other relevant information that will improve your chances of getting a job
References	the names of people (such as previous employers, teachers, and so on) who will be able to "put in a good word" for you

Exercise Set 14-4

A.   Provide the missing section titles (*Education, References,* and so on):

Résumé

Jean McDowell

201 Pine Street
Milwaukee, WI 55428
USA
Tel.: (414) 787-7878
E-mail: jean.mcdowell@sympatico.com

_____

  To find employment in the Milwaukee school system

_____

  B.A. in mathematics at the University of Wisconsin at Milwaukee
  High School Diploma, Kenosha, Wisconsin

_____

  Teacher's assistant in several elementary schools in Milwaukee
  Volunteer at Youth Center in Kenosha
  Tutored high school students for 2 years

_____

  Member of Mensa
  Hobbies include playing the violin

_____

  Available upon request

B.   Choose the appropriate answer, (a) or (b).

1. A résumé is also called a ...
   (a) curriculum vitae
   (b) summary

2. Under *Job Objective* you can indicate:
   (a) why you are applying for a job
   (b) what objectives you have in life

3. You should list all the places where you have worked under:
   (a) *References*
   (b) *Work Experience*

4. Under *Education* you would list:
   (a) your diplomas, degrees, and so on
   (b) your experiences at school

5. Under *Other Details* you would provide:
   (a) information that will improve your chances of getting the job
   (b) details about your hobbies

15

This and That

You can be a little ungrammatical if you come
from the right part of the country.

Robert Frost (1874–1963)

Dependent Clauses

1. Recall from Chapter 1 that a *clause* is a group of words containing a subject and a predicate. Clauses have been discussed in previous chapters. In this one, the remaining details with regard to clauses will be discussed. As you know, dependent clauses begin with words such as *that, which, where,* and so on:

   I do not know <u>where</u> Mary lives.
   I do not know <u>what</u> she does for a living.
   I do not know <u>why</u> she lives there.
   I do not know <u>whose</u> house that is.
   I do not know <u>how</u> she can live there.
   I do not know <u>when</u> she will live there.
   I do not know <u>whom</u> she called yesterday.

2. There are three main types of dependent clauses: noun, adjective, and adverb. A *noun clause* is any dependent clause that can function as a subject or predicate:

As subject:

<u>Where Mary lives</u> is very nice.

As predicate:

I do not know <u>where Mary lives</u>.

Agreement

The verb in a dependent clause agrees with the subject of the clause:

where she lives
where they live

However, as the subject of a sentence, the clause always takes a singular main verb even if its own verb is plural:

Where she lives is irrelevant.
Where they live is irrelevant.

---

3. As a response to a yes / no question (Chapter 7), a noun clause is generally introduced by *whether* or *if*:

Will Mary come to the party?   *I do not know <u>whether</u> she will come.*
     I am not sure <u>if</u> she will come.

4. A noun clause can also be introduced by *that* (known as a *complementizer*):

As subject:

<u>*That Mary loves French*</u> *is obvious.*

As predicate:

It is obvious <u>that Mary loves French</u>.

5. If the clause functions as a predicate, *that* is sometimes omitted:

We know that she lives there.
or
We know she lives there.

6. A subjunctive verb is used as a noun when the verb or adjective in the main clause expresses advisability, urgency, or importance:

She insists that we always <u>be</u> on time.
It is important that he <u>be told</u> the truth.

7. The subjunctive form of any verb is equivalent to its simple infinitive:

> **Verbs and Adjectives Requiring the Subjunctive**
>
> Verbs:
>   *advise*
>   *ask*
>   *demand*
>   *insist*
>   *propose*
>   *recommend*
>   *request*
>   *suggest*
>
> Adjectives:
>   *it is essential (that)*
>   *it is imperative (that)*
>   *it is important (that)*
>   *it is critical (that)*
>   *it is necessary (that)*
>   *it is vital (that)*

Indicative

We <u>are</u> on time.
He <u>comes</u> early.

Subjunctive

It is vital that we <u>be</u> on time.
It is vital that he <u>come</u> early.

8. There are also imperfect and pluperfect forms of the subjunctive constructed with the formulas *were + to + infinitive* (imperfect) and *were + to + have + past participle* (pluperfect). These are used in "counterfactual clauses," usually introduced by *if*, when the main clause verb is in the conditional. In current American English, the indicative is used in place of the subjunctive in such clauses:

If you were to go to Rome, you would see the Pantheon. / If you go to Rome, you would see the Pantheon.

If you were to have gone to Paris (but you didn't), you would have seen the Eiffel Tower. / If you had gone to Paris (but you didn't), you would have seen the Eiffel Tower.

9. An *adjective clause* (also called a *relative clause*) is a dependent clause that modifies a noun, giving further information about it. It is introduced by a relative pronoun (Chapter 5):

   You must always thank the persons <u>who help you out</u>.
   The ideas <u>that you are proposing</u> are not new.

10. Adjective clauses can also function as the objects of prepositions. In this case only *whom* (for person antecedents) and *which* (for nonperson antecedents) can be used as relative pronouns if the preposition begins the adjective clause:

    She is the one <u>about whom</u> I spoke.
    She is the person <u>to whom</u> I gave the money.

    The music <u>to which</u> we listened last night was very enjoyable.
    The subject <u>about which</u> he spoke is truly interesting.

11. Notice that if the antecedent refers to a place, the appropriate relative pronoun is *where*; and if it refers to time, it is *when*:

    The resort <u>where</u> we will be going is not far from here.
    The month <u>when</u> we will be going has not yet been decided.

12. Commas are used only when the adjective clause gives additional information:

    The doctor who works in that hospital is my best friend (the clause is necessary to identify the *doctor*).

    Doctor Smith, who works in that hospital, is my best friend (the clause gives additional information, because we know the name of the doctor).

13. An adjective clause may also contain an expression of quantity (*some of, many of, a bit of,* and so on). Only *whom, which,* and *whose* can be used as relative pronouns in this case:

    My friends, many of whom live far away, generally call me on weekends.
    They discussed a lot of topics, a number of which were rather boring.

14. Adjective clauses can be shortened by eliminating the relative pronoun and the verb *be*:

The boy who is sitting next to me is my brother.
or
The boy sitting next to me is my brother.

The book that is on the desk is mine.
or
The book on the desk is mine.

The ideas that are being presented in the book are rather good.
or
The ideas presented in the book are rather good.

15. When the verb *be* doesn't appear in the clause, change the verb to the present participle:

The people who sat next to me at dinner were nice.
or
The people sitting next to me at dinner were nice.

16. An *adverb clause* is a dependent clause that functions as an adverb:

We went to many good restaurants <u>when we were in Chicago</u>.
He studied a lot <u>because he wanted to get into that private school</u>.

17. An adverb clause can precede or follow the main clause. When it precedes, a comma is required:

When we were in Chicago, we went to many restaurants.
Because he wanted to get into that private school, he studied a lot.

Words Introducing Adverb Clauses

Time:
> after, before, when, while, as, as soon as, since, until, by the time, once, as long as, whenever, every time that

Cause and effect:
> because, now that, since

Contrast:
> even though, although, though, while, whereas

Condition:
> if, unless, only if, whether or not, even if, in case, in the event that

18. Adverb clauses can be reduced in a way similar to adjective clauses, but only if the subjects of the dependent and independent clauses are the same. The verb, moreover, is changed to the present participle:

    While I walked, I ran into my best friend.
    or
    While walking, I ran into my best friend.

    Before she left for work, she had a cup of coffee.
    or
    Before leaving for work, she had a cup of coffee.

    Since Mary came to the United States, she has made many friends.
    or
    Since coming to the United States, Mary has made many friends.

    But the following cannot be shortened:

    While she walked, I ran into my best friend.
    Before she left for work, I had a cup of coffee.

19. Sometimes, *while* can be omitted if it starts the sentence:

    While walking, I ran into my best friend.
    or
    Walking, I ran into my best friend.

Exercise Set 15-1

A. Provide the missing words (*when, that,* and so on).

1. _____ we were in Florida, we went to the beach a lot.
2. _____ he wanted to win first prize, he practiced a lot.
3. My cousins, many of _____ live nearby, generally call me on weekends.
4. It is important _____ he study a lot for the exam.
5. She is the person _____ knows which movie we are supposed to see.
6. The book, _____ title I have forgotten, is on the first shelf.
7. The idea _____ we have been discussing is an old one.

B. Provide an equivalent.

> *Example:* While walking, I ran into my cousin.
> *Walking, I ran into my cousin.*

1. Before they left for the movies, they had a long conversation.
2. Since they came to San Francisco, they have made many friends.
3. The people who sat next to me at the opera were very noisy.
4. The woman who is sitting next to me is my mother.
5. The CD that is playing right now is by Frank Sinatra.
6. The ideas that are being discussed on that program are rather boring.

Quoted and Reported Speech

1. Recall from Chapter 1 that the term *quoted speech* refers to the reproduction of words exactly as they were spoken by someone. In writing, quotation marks ("____") are used:

> *She said, "My brother loves his dog."*
> *"My bother loves his dog," she said.*
> *"My brother," she said, "loves his dog."*

2. The most common quotation verbs are *say, tell, ask, add, announce, answer, comment, suggest. whisper, confess, respond, remark, reply, explain,* and *inquire:*

> *She added, "Where are they?"*
> *They announced, "We are coming as well."*
> *"That is incorrect," he suggested.*
> *"My career," he explained, "is simply wonderful."*

Punctuation

If the quoted speech is to be divided, use a comma after the first part.

Quotation marks are placed at the beginning and at the end of a complete quote, no matter where it occurs. The end punctuation mark is generally put before the second quotation mark.

The first word in a completely quoted sentence begins with a capital letter, no matter where it occurs.

If a question or exclamation mark is inside the quotation no other punctuation mark is used after it:

> *She asked, "Where is he?"*
> *"Where is he?" she asked.*
> *She said, "Be careful!"*

(*Note:* The verbs *speak* and *talk* are not reporting verbs!)

3. *Reported speech* involves reporting what was said. No quotation marks are used. The reported speech is phrased in the form of a noun clause (see page 257):

Quoted speech	Reported speech
"I love math."	He said (that) he loved math.
"We went to the movies."	They said (that) they went to the movies.

4. Note that the subject of the reported speech (in both the main and the subordinate clauses) refers to the speaker(s):

Speaker	Reported speech
I (the actual reporter)	I said (that) I loved math.
you (the one you are addressing)	You said (that) you loved math.
he / she / Mary (anyone else)	He / She / Mary ... said (that) he / she / ... loved math.
we	We said (that) we loved math.
they	They said (that) they loved math.

5. If the reporting verb is in the simple past, the verb in the noun clause is usually changed. In general, to report speech, change the tense of the noun clause verb to a tense that is past in relation to the verb in the quotation. Here are a few examples:

Quoted speech	Reported speech
"I <u>eat</u> meat often."	He said (that) he <u>ate</u> meat often.
"I <u>have eaten</u> meat."	He said (that) he <u>had eaten</u> meat.
"I <u>may</u> eat meat."	He said (that) he <u>might</u> eat meat.
"I <u>have</u> to eat meat."	He said (that) he <u>had</u> to eat meat.
"I <u>am going</u> to eat meat."	He said (that) he <u>was going</u> to eat meat.

6. There are exceptions to this general rule. Certain past tense modal verbs, such as *should, ought to,* and *might* are not changed:

Quoted speech	Reported speech
"I should eat meat more often."	He said (that) he should eat meat more often.
"I might eat meat more often."	He said (that) he might eat meat more often.

7. A tense change is optional if you are reporting something right away:

Immediate reporting	**Later reporting**
"He said that he eats / ate meat often."	*He said (that) he ate meat often.*
"They said that they are / were coming."	*They said (that) they were coming.*

Exercise Set 15-2

A. Change to reported speech.

Example: John said, "I'm coming too."
John said that he was coming too.

1. The boy remarked, "I watch TV a lot."
2. She responded, "I have not eaten anything."
3. I replied, "I may eat later."
4. Jane commented, "I have to get up early."
5. They added, "We are going to go out just the same."
6. Jill confessed, "I should work out more often."

B. Now change to quoted speech.

Example: Mary said that she was tired.
Mary said, "I am tired."

1. My friend said (that) he went out a lot.
2. Mary responded (that) she had not seen that movie.
3. She replied (that) she might call later.
4. They complained (that) they had to work all day.
5. They added (that) they were going to speak out just the same.
6. My sister confessed (that) she should study a lot more.

Variation

1. With a few exceptions, the type of language discussed in this book is what linguists and grammarians call *standard American English*. This is the type of English used in all kinds of official or formal situations.

2. There are many variant forms of language, known as *dialects*, that you will be exposed to as you use the language to interact with others. These are characterized above all else by a type of vocabulary called *slang*, which is designed to create and reinforce a specific group's identity.

3. But slang is not limited to dialect speech. Standard American English is constantly absorbing slang expressions, such as *glitzy* (gaudy) and *hype* (advertising that relies on gimmicks or tricks).

4. People use slang more often in speaking than in writing, and more often with friends than with strangers. Slang thus resembles colloquialisms, which are expressions used in everyday conversation but not considered appropriate for formal speech or writing.

5. Unlike colloquialisms, which can be understood by most people, many slang expressions are used by only a certain segment of society or by people with a specific occupation. In a hospital, a physician may be called to the emergency room *stat* (quickly) because a patient has *flatlined* (lost all heart functions). Young people often use slang to differentiate themselves from the adult world.

6. The type of slang used by specific occupational groups is known as *jargon*. Sometimes, jargon spreads to society at large. Expressions such as *ham it up* (to overact) and *turkey* (failure), for instance, come from theater jargon.

7. The increasing popularity of the Internet has spread into society at large a great deal of the jargon employed by computer users, including *cyber-* (dealing with computers and the Internet), *snail mail* (written messages delivered by the postal service), *hacker* (an expert computer programmer perhaps involved in illegal activities), *flaming* (a hostile response from a user), and *spamming* (sending numerous unsolicited messages to users).

8. In the United States, there are three major dialect types: (1) Northern, also called Eastern or New England; (2) Southern; and (3) Midland, also known as Western or Midwestern. Many local dialects exist within these main types.

9. The Northern dialect is spoken mainly in New York and New England. Some characteristics of Northern pronunciation include dropping the /r/ sound (*car* pronounced /kah/), and using the short /o/ instead of the open /ɔ/ (*fog* = /fɔg/).

10. The Southern dialect is spoken mainly in the southern states. Some of its features include loss of the /r/ sound, use of the broad /a/ (*time* = /ta^{h}m/), and use of a short /ɨ/ for /e/ before a nasal sound (*pen* = /pɨ^{h}n/).

11. The Midland dialect is spoken in Pennsylvania, West Virginia, and most states west of the Appalachian Mountains. This dialect is sometimes considered the standard form of American English because it is spoken over the largest geographic region. Pronunciation characteristics of the Midland dialect include use of the /r/ sound in all word positions, use of the open /ɔ/ for short /o/, and use of a long /ay/ in the word *time*.

12. In this book, you have been exposed to American English. There are other kinds of English, such as, for example, British and Canadian English. The most striking difference between these is probably pronunciation, although there are some vocabulary and spelling differences:

American spelling	British spelling
color	*colour*
center	*centre*
analyze	*analyse*

American vocabulary	British vocabulary
mail	*post*
gasoline	*petrol*
elevator	*lift*
subway	*underground*

13. Variation can also occur on a social level. Generally speaking, this involves levels of *formality*. As you have seen throughout this book, a distinction has been made between *formal* and *informal* speech. The former is used to show deference, politeness, or simply a certain style. The latter is used to show friendliness and a feeling of closeness.

14. Formality often involves the choice of words:

Formal	Informal
abode	*house, place*
alcoholic beverage	*drink, booze*
offspring	*children, kids*
dollars	*bucks*

15. In formal language, clipped or abbreviated words tend to be avoided:

Formal	Informal
laboratory	*lab*
advertisement	*ad*
newspaper	*paper*
good-bye	*bye*
hello	*hi*

Exercise Set 15-3

A.   Change from formal to informal.

1. abode
2. laboratory
3. advertisement
4. alcoholic beverage
5. newspaper
6. offspring
7. dollars
8. good-bye
9. hello

B. True (T) or false (F)?

_____ 1. Standard American English is used in all kinds of official or formal situations.

_____ 2. Variant forms of a language are known as dialects.

_____ 3. Slang speech is designed to create and reinforce a specific group's identity.

_____ 4. The type of slang used by specific occupational groups is known as jargon.

_____ 5. People use slang more often in writing than in speaking.

Answers

Chapter 1

Exercise Set 1-1

A.
1. My friend is Italian.
2. Who is she?
3. Go away!
4. My friend and I speak Spanish.
5. Each person in my house drives an American car.
6. The elderly are not necessarily wise.
7. The people in this city are always friendly.
8. Speaking many languages is difficult.
9. The United States is a great country.
10. Our dog, as well as our cat, is very friendly.
11. Yes, do it right away!
12. She asked me, "Are you Spanish?"
13. She asked me if I were Spanish.
14. That pastry was eaten by Mary.

B.
1. *Alex* = subject
2. *is a great pianist* = predicate
3. *that I am too young to get married* = dependent clause
4. *who rarely gets angry* = dependent clause
5. *Many people believe* = independent clause

C.
1. (b)
2. (a)
3. (a)
4. (a)

Exercise Set 1-2

A.

1. I
2. L
3. T
4. I
5. T (*give* can take both a direct and an indirect object)
6. T

B.

1. There are lots of people in this room.
2. There are many cars on the road today.
3. Debbie always sits on the sofa to watch TV.
4. I always wait for him after school.
5. She phones me every day.
6. He gave her a gift for her birthday.
7. We listened to the radio together.
8. It is (It's) correct, isn't it?

Exercise Set 1-3

A.

1. He did not do it.
2. Our friends have not seen that movie.
3. She will not be coming with us.
4. You should not eat so many sweets.
5. They are not coming to the movies.
6. He is not American.
7. I do not understand what you are talking about.

B.

1. My brother does not work at the library.
2. She cannot work at the library.
3. He does not go to Princeton.
4. I do not believe you.
5. My sister also did not believe you.
6. I may not do it.
7. I did not do it.

Exercise Set 1-4

A.
1. How are you feeling? / How are you?
2. Why isn't he going?
3. Is Alex your brother? / Isn't Alex your brother?
4. Are her friends coming to the party? / Aren't her friends coming to the party? / Are her friends not coming to the party?
5. Can you do it? / Can't you do it? / Can you not do it?
6. Does he watch TV every night? / Doesn't he watch TV every night? / Does he not watch TV every night?
7. Does she like that sitcom? / Doesn't she like that sitcom? / Does she not like that sitcom?
8. When are they arriving?
9. Which house do you prefer?
10. Where did they go last night?
11. What is it?
12. Did he eat all of it? / Didn't he eat all of it? / Did he not eat all of it?

B.
1. (a)
2. (b)
3. (b)
4. (b)
5. (a)
6. (a)

Exercise Set 1-5

A.
1. The person who lives next to you is my cousin.
2. Did you go to the movies last night?
3. Juan and Francesca speak Japanese.
4. I adore the book that / which I am reading right now.
5. It makes me happy that he calls all the time.
6. While he sleeps, I usually read.
7. Watching movies is a great way to spend an evening together.

B.
1. (a)
2. (a)
3. (b)
4. (a)
5. (b)
6. (a)

C.
1. The person who is talking is my good friend.
2. Mary or John should go to the party, but not both.
3. He got sick, for / because he got a cold walking in the rain.
4. The book that / which you borrowed belongs to my sister.
5. He is not well, but he is going out just the same.
6. I like the house that you are building.

Exercise Set 1-6

A.
1. We drove all day, even though it was raining heavily.
2. They are still friends, even though / although they argue a lot.
3. It is a nice day; the sun is shining. / It is a nice day, because the sun is shining.
4. I am her brother, even though / although I do not look like her.

B.
1. (a)
2. (b)
3. (a)
4. (a)

Chapter 2

Exercise Set 2-1

A.
1. Where is Ms. Jones going?
2. I love tennis.

3. Did you go to the University of Florida?
4. She speaks English very well, even though she is not American.
5. Have you ever met Dr. Smith? Isn't he Jewish?
6. I go downtown every Saturday with my friends.
7. Aren't you of Russian origin?

B.
1. (a)
2. (b)
3. (a)
4. (b)
5. (a)
6. (a)

C.

Proper	Count	Noncount	Borrowed
Alex	bike	air	blitz
America	car	bread	gusto
Cadillac	coin	cash	machismo
Idaho	dog	checkers	opera
Japan	friend	chess	pizza
Kentucky	game	fun	ravioli
Paris	key	gold	salami
Sarah	poem	mathematics	soprano
the Mississippi	shoe	rice	spaghetti
the Rockies	tulip	work	zucchini

Exercise Set 2-2

A.

	Male		Female
1.	Gerald	1.	Geraldine
2.	brother	2.	sister
3.	waiter	3.	waitress / female waiter
4.	male professor	4.	female professor
5.	male friend	5.	female friend
6.	Robert	6.	Roberta
7.	dad	7.	mom
8.	chairman	8.	chairwoman
9.	spokesman	9.	spokeswoman
10.	Doctor	10.	Doctor
11.	Mr.	11.	Mrs. / Ms. / Miss

B.
1. (a)
2. (b)
3. (a)
4. (b)
5. (b)
6. (b)

Exercise Set 2-3

A.
1. babies
2. potatoes
3. heroes
4. desks
5. branches
6. toys
7. chiefs
8. attorneys
9. roofs
10. lives
11. knives
12. bridges

B.
1. tooth
2. mouse
3. phenomenon
4. child
5. ox
6. species
7. foot
8. leaf
9. cactus
10. index
11. stimulus
12. radius
13. medium
14. analysis
15. thesis

C.

1. sheep
2. deer
3. nuclei
4. dormitories
5. shelves
6. halves
7. loaves
8. scarves
9. spies
10. cherries
11. traffic
12. patience
13. scissors
14. pants
15. pharmacies

Exercise Set 2-4

A.

1. a dollar's worth
2. the book's success
3. my brother's, sister's, and friend's favorite movie
4. five-week pay
5. the fox's cunning
6. the vegetable drink
7. the office party
8. Jean's friend
9. the girl's dress
10. New Year's Day
11. several three-minute exercises
12. my twenty-year-old cousin

B.

1. the girls' friends
2. the mothers' routine
3. the witnesses' story
4. the men's washroom
5. the children's puzzle
6. the leaves' color

Exercise Set 2-5

A.
1. *il* = prefix, *legal* = root
2. *friend* = root, *ly* = suffix
3. *un* = prefix, *friend* = root, *ly* = suffix
4. *mis* = prefix, *calculate* = root, *tion* = suffix
5. *dis* = prefix, *belief* = root
6. *believe* = root, *able* = suffix
7. *re* = prefix, *cover* = root, *able* = suffix

B.
1. (b)
2. (a)
3. (a)
4. (a)
5. (a)

Exercise Set 2-6

A.
1. *green* = adjective, *house* = noun
2. *family* = noun, *planning* = verb
3. *birth* = noun, *control* = noun
4. *sun* = noun, *glasses* = noun
5. *make* = verb, *up* = preposition
6. *answering* = verb, *machine* = noun
7. *in* = preposition, *put* = verb
8. *walk* = verb, *out* = preposition
9. *screw* = noun, *driver* = noun

B.
1. headaches
2. notebooks
3. outputs
4. railroads
5. managing editors
6. bookstores
7. sisters-in-law

Chapter 3

Exercise Set 3-1

A.
1. *the* = definite article
2. *an* = indefinite article
3. *some* = quantifier
4. *this* = demonstrative
5. *your* = possessive
6. *any* = quantifier
7. *several* = quantifier

B.
1. (a)
2. (b)
3. (a)
4. (b)
5. (a)
6. (b)

Exercise Set 3-2

A.
1. a girl
2. an intelligent girl
3. a man
4. an American woman
5. a house
6. an hour
7. a late hour
8. an underdog

B.
1. I would love a piece of chocolate cake, no matter what kind it is.
2. I would love the rice that you made yesterday.
3. I need a new TV set.
4. The TV set you bought yesterday is a plasma set, isn't it?
5. What a great deal that was!

6. I need new shoes.
7. Rice is good for you, generally speaking.
8. The rice is tastier than the pasta.
9. Do you know the doctor who lives next door to us?
10. "Good morning, Doctor Banning."
11. Doctor Smith lives next door to us.
12. The books I gave you yesterday are very good.
13. Books are important learning tools.
14. I love Italian food.
15. Do you play the piano?
16. Have you ever been to Germany?
17. No, but I have been to the Philippines.
18. Have you ever seen San Francisco Bay?
19. Today is September fifteenth. / Today is September the fifteenth.
20. Today is the twenty-first of September.
21. I love studying geometry.
22. Are you going to the movies tonight?
23. I often go to church on Sundays.

Exercise Set 3-3

A.
1. those boys
2. these women
3. this idea
4. that car
5. those arguments
6. this leaf
7. these mistakes

B.
1. Those books over there belong to my sister.
2. These books here belong to me.
3. Who is that man walking on the other side of the street?
4. I do not recognize this person right here in the photograph.
5. I would like to eat all of that rice over there, but I am too full.
6. I have made that same mistake over and over.
7. I am distancing myself from those ideas because they have become old-fashioned.

Exercise Set 3-4

A.
1. Mary, where do you think you lost your purse?
2. Mary always hands in her assignments on time.
3. Mary's brother, on the other hand, always hands in his assignments late.
4. That dog is always licking its paws.
5. We are not sure if our parents will agree to let us go out tonight.
6. Where are those two people? They left their briefcases on the table.
7. Everyone should be thankful for his / her / their good fortune.

B.
1. (b)
2. (b)
3. (a)
4. (b)
5. (a)
6. (a)
7. (a)
8. (b)

Exercise Set 3-5

A.
1. I would like some / a little water, please.
2. May I have some / a few books / several books?
3. He ate most of the cake, but not all of it.
4. We bought many / several books yesterday.
5. Some of those clothes are new.
6. Some of that equipment is new.
7. One of the books is mine.
8. Each of those DVDs is new.
9. I will never eat any meat again.
10. I do not have any / enough money.
11. Every / Each morning we read the newspaper.
12. I know that girl. But who is the other girl?

B.
1. (a)
2. (b)

3. (a)
4. (a)
5. (a)
6. (a)
7. (b)
8. (b)

Chapter 4

Exercise Set 4-1

A.
1. I bought a brand new plasma TV set yesterday.
2. They are very bright children.
3. The sweater and the purse are blue.
4. Sarah is an intelligent person who always scores high on IQ tests.
5. My grandson is a very generous person who helps people in need.
6. That test might seem easy but it is actually quite difficult.
7. These shoes are becoming tattered.
8. The chocolates taste very sweet.
9. That symphony sounds beautiful.
10. She looks stunning in that dress.

B.
1. joyous / joyful
2. critical
3. workable / working
4. sensible / sensitive
5. creamy
6. pleasurable
7. penniless

Exercise Set 4-2

A.
1. a singing nun
2. a listening device
3. a reading light
4. a playing field

5. a loving friend
6. a knowing gesture
7. a moving poem

B.
1. self-centered people
2. a well-known politician
3. an absent-minded professor
4. a built-in device
5. a walk-in clinic
6. good-humored people

Exercise Set 4-3

A.
1. elegantly
2. nearly
3. sincerely
4. lovely
5. lately
6. palpably
7. luckily
8. greedily
9. initially
10. wonderfully

B.
1. They're coming after / before five o'clock.
2. Did you do that again even though I told you not to?
3. They should make it on time because they are almost finished working.
4. He was already up by 5 A.M.
5. I will also try to come, if I have time.
6. There was so much fog that we could barely / hardly / scarcely see the road.
7. I ran into her yesterday by chance.
8. By now you should know what to expect.
9. It is too early to get up. I went to bed very late last night.
10. She will go instead of him.
11. What time is it now?

12. We did it only to impress them.
13. I'll try to get to it in a little while / right away / soon.
14. Come at four. I'll be ready then.
15. I like baseball; and my grandson likes it too.

Exercise Set 4-4

A.

Positive	Comparative of majority	Comparative of minority	Superlative of majority	Superlative of minority
tough	tougher	less tough	(the) toughest	(the) least tough
useful	more useful	less useful	(the) most useful	(the) least useful
tall	taller	less tall	(the) tallest	(the) least tall
timid	more timid	less timid	(the) most timid	(the) least timid
bad	worse	(not applicable)	(the) worst	(not applicable)
far	farther	less far	(the) farthest	(the) least far
well	better	less well	(the) best	(the) least well
good	better	less good	(the) best	(the) least good
little	less	(not applicable)	(the) least	(not applicable)

B.
1. Alex is the smartest person in the world.
2. I love the English language as much as you do, if not more.
3. Sarah is the most intelligent person I know.
4. Pluto is big; Neptune is bigger; Jupiter is the biggest.
5. Calculus is difficult; probability theory is less difficult; geometry is the least difficult.
6. You are the best friend I have ever had. You are absolutely great!

Chapter 5

Exercise Set 5-1

A.
1. That belongs to my daughter.
2. Those are brand new.
3. This has lots of memory.
4. These are too long to fill out.
5. Why did you buy that?
6. What is this?

B.
1. Mine is new.
2. Theirs are going abroad this year.
3. Hers speaks English very well.
4. His is a good one.
5. Yours needs some repair.
6. Ours is full of weeds.

Exercise Set 5-2

A.
1. John and I are going out together.
2. Who is that man? He is my brother.
3. My sister always calls when she has free time.
4. They are our parents. / We are their parents.
5. Where is my watch? It is on the desk.
6. Mary calls me every evening.
7. Do it for us!
8. I spoke to him yesterday.
9. That belongs to her.
10. Who are they?
11. Speak to them.

B.
1. (a)
2. (a)
3. (b)
4. (a)
5. (a)
6. (b)

Exercise Set 5-3

A.
1. My cousin and his fiancée really adore each other.
2. He always does those things himself.
3. The workers in that company support one another.
4. Do you live by yourself?
5. One should always look after oneself.
6. The situation will work itself out.

7. She considers herself to be beautiful.
8. We tried to do it ourselves, but couldn't.
9. They worry only about themselves.
10. I'm not sure I can do it by myself.

B.

Subject	Direct object	Indirect object	Possessive	Reflexive
I	me	(to) me	mine	myself
they	them	(to) them	theirs	themselves
we	us	(to) us	ours	ourselves
you	you	(to) you	yours	yourself
he	him	(to) him	his	himself
you	you	(to) you	yours	yourselves
she	her	(to) her	hers	herself
it	it	(to) it	its	itself

Exercise Set 5-4

A.
1. The woman who is reading the newspaper is my sister.
2. They are the people who are coming to our party.
3. My car, which is brand new, is always giving me problems.
4. The book that I read yesterday was better than the one I read two weeks ago.
5. The jacket that I bought yesterday is much too tight.
6. I love the piano piece that you are performing tonight.
7. Those who believe him will soon find out that they have been duped.
8. She bought only what she needed.
9. What is really shocking is that they didn't even mention a word about the incident.
10. To whom did you speak yesterday?
11. The shelf on which I put the book is rather high.
12. She is the woman whom I met last night.
13. That is a nation whose influence over international affairs has been greatly reduced.
14. The song, whose style is very jazzy, is typical of that genre.

B.
1. (a)
2. (b)

3. (b)
4. (a)
5. (b)
6. (a)

Exercise Set 5-5

A.
1. They drink quite a lot.
2. No one speaks Spanish here.
3. Everyone is going to Italy this year.
4. Some work in the evening, but many / most work in the daytime.
5. Many know that.
6. Anybody who wants to come is welcome.
7. Anything is better than nothing.
8. Something is bothering her.
9. Wherever you go, I will follow you.
10. Some will study in the United States; others, instead, will study in their own countries.
11. There are many things to do.
12. Hello there. How are you?

B.
1. (a)
2. (b)
3. (a)
4. (b)
5. (a)
6. (b)
7. (a)

Chapter 6

Exercise Set 6-1

A.
1. There are about / around fifty miles to go before we reach Chicago.
2. The temperature has been above / below normal the entire winter.

3. The store is just across / around the street.
4. Let's go to the movies after dinner, not before.
5. It's just a few minutes after / before five.
6. Do not lean against the fence; we just painted it.
7. The sidewalk runs all along the avenue.
8. He is now among the very wealthy.
9. Our house is just around the corner.
10. I usually go to bed around / at ten.
11. I'll meet you at the movies.
12. I'll see you at / before / after seven o'clock.
13. She's really good at piano-playing.
14. They came at / after / before ten o'clock.
15. He sat behind her throughout school.
16. Everyone is behind schedule, unfortunately.
17. Such behavior is beneath you.
18. It is beneath me to beg.
19. He has earned a place among / with the best thinkers in America.
20. You must choose between him and her.
21. I prepared lunch for you.
22. We walked and walked for hours.
23. She was named for / after a Biblical character.
24. I'm free from five o'clock on.
25. Don't you know right from wrong any longer?
26. They're both born in September.
27. That man has spent his entire life in politics.
28. You can pay for it in cash.
29. You're in for a big surprise.
30. They have always lived like privileged people.
31. They are staying at a hotel near Chicago.
32. We live near the mall.
33. Our home is a few miles from here.
34. That was very nice of her.
35. I think highly of her musicianship.

B.
  1. (z)
  2. (y)
  3. (x)
  4. (w)
  5. (v)

6. (q)
7. (r)
8. (s)
9. (t)
10. (u)
11. (l)
12. (m)
13. (n)
14. (o)
15. (p)
16. (k)
17. (j)
18. (i)
19. (h)
20. (g)
21. (f)
22. (b)
23. (c)
24. (d)
25. (e)
26. (a)

C.
1. (b)
2. (a)
3. (a)
4. (b)
5. (b)
6. (a)

Exercise Set 6-2

A.
1. Going out for a walk in the pouring rain is not a good idea.
2. Let's meet on Wednesday. OK?
3. We always go out on Saturdays.
4. We're going on vacation soon.
5. They live in San Francisco.
6. I am staying in the country as a tourist.
7. He's working in the garage.

8. She's getting in the van as we speak.
9. I'll see you in the afternoon.
10. We're going in June.
11. He just got on the plane.

B.

1. He goes to the mall on Saturdays.
2. They are leaving on Friday.
3. I'll call you in the morning.
4. I do not like traveling in a thunderstorm.
5. The game will be on in the afternoon.

Exercise Set 6-3

A.

1. We decided to go out after we had finished dinner.
2. Although / Even though / Though I like music, I cannot listen to that particular song any longer.
3. Although / Even though / Though he finds math easy, he prefers to be anything but a mathematician.
4. I stumbled on the sidewalk as I ran home.
5. Our winters are cold, as everyone knows.
6. Alex loves math and he loves music.
7. Mark or Mary should do that, not you.
8. The pants are tight, but comfortable.
9. I am not well, so I'm not coming.
10. I am not bored, nor am I tired.
11. I always watch baseball because I like it.
12. Call me before you leave.
13. If that is the case, what should I do?
14. Although / Even though / Though she may not succeed, she will still try.
15. We'll call you when we get there.

B.

1. Both Jim and his friend play baseball.
2. He is good not only at music but also in sports.
3. She will grow up to be either a doctor or a lawyer.

4. That song is neither melodious nor rhythmic.
5. It was pouring rain, but I went swimming anyway.

Exercise Set 6-4

A.
  1. (c)
  2. (a)
  3. (d)
  4. (e)
  5. (b)

B.
  1. Oh!
  2. Ouch!
  3. No matter!
  4. Huh?
  5. How come?
  6. Ah!

Exercise Set 6-5

A.
  1. I always work through lunch, and therefore I am always hungry at the end of the day.
  2. Few know as much as you do; thus they expect you to take the lead.
  3. Yes, I'll do it.
  4. No, she's not coming.
  5. There's room in the car for only one other person.
  6. The essay is difficult; however, it's worth reading.
  7. Maybe I should go too.
  8. Although you are right, you should nevertheless keep quiet about it.

B.
  1. (a)
  2. (a)
  3. (a)
  4. (a)
  5. (b)

Chapter 7

Exercise Set 7-1

A.
1. Is he here?
2. Are they your relatives?
3. Is she coming to Florida?
4. Are they going to Europe?
5. Has he heard that piece before?
6. Had they come to the party?
7. Can I have some coffee?
8. Will they be coming as well?
9. May I suggest something?
10. Does she go to Harvard?
11. Do they go to Chicago often?
12. Did he pass the exam?
13. Did they understand your instructions?

B.
1. (e)
2. (d)
3. (g)
4. (b)
5. (a)
6. (c)
7. (h)
8. (f)
9. (j)
10. (i)
11. (l)
12. (k)

C.
1. She's American, isn't she?
2. They're always late, aren't they?
3. You study a lot, don't you?
4. He's here, isn't he?
5. They should come too, shouldn't they?

6. That CD is yours, isn't it?
7. Everything is OK, isn't it?
8. These belong here, don't they?
9. Those are your relatives, aren't they?
10. Many showed up late, didn't they?

Exercise Set 7-2

A.
1. He is not / isn't an old friend.
2. I was not / wasn't watching TV when you called.
3. He has not / hasn't played that before.
4. I would not / wouldn't agree.
5. He may not come.
6. Nobody said that.
7. She does not / doesn't live in France.
8. He did not / didn't study for the exam.
9. Doesn't his friend live in Los Angeles?
10. Isn't Mary coming?
11. Hasn't he eaten yet?

B.
1. (a)
2. (a)
3. (a)
4. (a)
5. (b)
6. (a)
7. (a)
8. (b)
9. (a)

Exercise Set 7-3

A.
1. blameless
2. unsure
3. pseudonym
4. nonissue
5. misinform

6. immoral
7. improbable
8. irresponsible
9. illegal
10. incorrect
11. dissimilar
12. antisocial

B.
1. underpaid
2. biannual(ly)
3. redo
4. pro-democracy
5. preview
6. postwar
7. overwork
8. ex-schoolmate
9. autobiography

Chapter 8

Exercise Set 8-1

A.
1. (b)
2. (a)
3. (a)
4. (a)
5. (a)
6. (a)
7. (b)
8. (b)
9. (b)
10. (a)
11. (a)
12. (a)

B.

1. He does not / doesn't speak English.
2. She does not / doesn't have lots of money
3. They do not / don't go to Europe every year.
4. I do not / don't play the piano.
5. He does not / doesn't play the cello.
6. My friends do not / don't live in New York.

Exercise Set 8-2

A.

1. played
2. cared
3. learned
4. finished
5. eaten
6. heard
7. fled
8. seen
9. stopped
10. jabbed
11. tanned
12. rained
13. dumped
14. opened
15. referred
16. studied
17. tried
18. had
19. been
20. gone

B.

1. The student has studied already.
2. He has done that already.
3. I have taken the bus many times.
4. She has enjoyed Beethoven's music all her life.
5. You have stayed with us often.
6. We have learned to use good grammar in school.

C.
1. Hasn't he spoken to the professor?
2. Haven't you done it?
3. Haven't we said that?
4. Hasn't she taken it?
5. Haven't they painted their house?

Exercise Set 8-3

A.
1. I ate
2. you were
3. he had
4. they were
5. I was
6. we were
7. Mary was
8. they saw
9. I took
10. we heard

B.
1. We did not / didn't agree with you.
2. She did not / didn't speak to me.
3. He did not / didn't say that.
4. I did not / didn't hear it.
5. You did not / didn't go downtown.
6. He was not / wasn't late.
7. You were not / weren't there.

C.
1. Did she see you yesterday?
2. Did he have a toothache?
3. Did they do it already?
4. Was he there too?
5. Were they in the house yesterday?
6. Did he see them too?
7. Did she sing a new tune?

Exercise Set 8-4

A.

1. (b)
2. (a)
3. (b)
4. (b)
5. (b)

B.

	Simple present	Present perfect	Simple past	Pluperfect
reply	(he) replies	(I) have replied	(she) replied	(we) had replied
say	(he) says	(I) have said	(she) said	(we) had said
go	(he) goes	(I) have gone	(she) went	(we) had gone
do	(he) does	(I) have done	(she) did	(we) had done
finish	(he) finishes	(I) have finished	(she) finished	(we) had finished
reach	(he) reaches	(I) have reached	(she) reached	(we) had reached
be	(he) is	(I) have been	(she) was	(we) had been
have	(he) has	(I) have had	(she) had	(we) had had
love	(he) loves	(I) have loved	(she) loved	(we) had loved
rub	(he) rubs	(I) have rubbed	(she) rubbed	(we) had rubbed
gain	(he) gains	(I) have gained	(she) gained	(we) had gained
open	(he) opens	(I) have opened	(she) opened	(we) had opened
see	(he) sees	(I) have seen	(she) saw	(we) had seen
sing	(he) sings	(I) have sung	(she) sang	(we) had sung
speak	(he) speaks	(I) have spoken	(she) spoke	(we) had spoken
take	(he) takes	(I) have taken	(she) took	(we) had taken

Exercise Set 8-5

A.

1. Mark, drink all the milk!
2. Mark, come early!
3. Mark, be silent!
4. Mark, speak English!
5. Mr. and Mrs. Smith, watch the new TV show!
6. Mr. and Mrs. Smith, go out!
7. Mr. and Mrs. Smith, finish the cake!

B.

1. Mark, don't drink all the milk!
2. Mark, don't come early!
3. Mark, don't be silent!
4. Mark, don't speak English!
5. Mr. and Mrs. Smith, don't watch the new TV show!
6. Mr. and Mrs. Smith, don't go out!
7. Mr. and Mrs. Smith, don't finish the cake!

Exercise Set 8-6

A.

	Present	Present perfect	Past	Pluperfect
lie	(he) is lying	(I) have been lying	(she) was lying	(we) had been lying
say	(he) is saying	(I) have been saying	(she) was saying	(we) had been saying
go	(he) is going	(I) have been going	(she) was going	(we) had been going
do	(he) is doing	(I) have been doing	(she) was doing	(we) had been doing
finish	(he) is finishing	(I) have been finishing	(she) was finishing	(we) had been finishing
reach	(he) is reaching	(I) have been reaching	(she) was reaching	(we) had been reaching
have	(he) is having	(I) have been having	(she) was having	(we) had been having
love	(he) is loving	(I) have been loving	(she) was loving	(we) had been loving
rub	(he) is rubbing	(I) have been rubbing	(she) was rubbing	(we) had been rubbing
gain	(he) is gaining	(I) have been gaining	(she) was gaining	(we) had been gaining
open	(he) is opening	(I) have been opening	(she) was opening	(we) had been opening
see	(he) is seeing	(I) have been seeing	(she) was seeing	(we) had been seeing
sing	(he) is singing	(I) have been singing	(she) was singing	(we) had been singing
speak	(he) is speaking	(I) have been speaking	(she) was speaking	(we) had been speaking
take	(he) is taking	(I) have been taking	(she) was taking	(we) had been taking

B.

1. (b)
2. (a)
3. (b)
4. (b)
5. (b)
6. (b)

Exercise Set 8-7

A.
1. She always enjoys herself at the movies.
2. Are you enjoying yourself?
3. To go willingly is to show strength.
4. She hopes to go / to be going to Spain next year.
5. I am lucky to be so successful.
6. They wanted to come early.
7. To have gone willingly is to have shown courage.
8. I am interested in learning more about grammar.
9. He always complains about eating out.
10. You must forgive me for speaking too candidly.
11. I am going to try to prevent you from smoking.
12. We look forward to being with you.
13. I am tired of working so hard.
14. He has succeeded in becoming rich.
15. She finished working early today.
16. Having eaten everything, we decided to go out.
17. I saw him walk / walking down the street.
18. It is impossible to learn English quickly.

B.
1. She promised not to be late.
2. You seem not to know much.
3. They are upset about not going to Europe.
4. Not exercising can lead to health problems.
5. I would not like to go there. / I would like to not go there.

Chapter 9

Exercise Set 9-1

A.
1. He can do it too.
2. Can / May / Might I be excused?
3. I could run faster when I was younger.
4. If we could help, we would.

5. May I come in?
6. Long may they live!
7. She said yesterday that they could / might not go on the trip.
8. Trees must have oxygen in order to survive.
9. If you must leave, do it quietly.
10. They won't come till much later.
11. You may not do that.
12. I should have gone to the mall with you.
13. He may be sleeping, so do not bother him.
14. He must have been playing Chopin. Who else could it have been?

B.
1. (a)
2. (a)
3. (b)
4. (a)
5. (a)
6. (a)
7. (a)
8. (b)

Exercise Set 9-2

A.
1. After you get home, we will have dinner.
2. As soon as he arrives, we will turn on the TV.
3. We will have eaten by the time he arrives.
4. I would go away to college next year, but I don't have enough money.
5. She would not go to that school if she had her way.
6. She would have gone to see that movie, but she was very busy.
7. I will definitely go with you to the movies tomorrow.
8. I would like to go with you, but I have no time.

B.
1. (a)
2. (b)
3. (a)
4. (a)
5. (b)

Exercise Set 9-3

Λ.
1. She is loved by Alex.
2. That novel is being read by my friend.
3. It has been done by me already.
4. She was called by Mary.
5. My favorite song was being sung by them.
6. She had been helped by us.
7. You will be taught by me.
8. She will have been called by your friends already.

B.
1. (b)
2. (a)
3. (b)
4. (a)
5. (b)
6. (b)

C.
1. Jack is married to Julie.
2. I was exposed to that idea many years ago.
3. They are related to my brother-in-law.
4. I am filled with joy.
5. She is done with working late.
6. It is always best to protect your family from danger.
7. Are you worried about your health?
8. Are you involved in music?

Chapter 10

Exercise Set 10-1

A.
1. Your style has always made for better communication.
2. They made off in a hurry upon seeing us arrive.
3. You need to make over that room.

4. Get your doctor to make you out a new prescription.
5. Why do you make up your face so much when you go out on a date?
6. Let's kiss and make up, OK?
7. Why do you always make those awful faces when I talk to you?
8. The robbers made off / away with a lot of money.
9. We're going to have to make do on less money.
10. We are always trying to make ends meet with what we have.
11. I caught them making eyes at each other.
12. Why are you always making fun of me?
13. He finally made it as a successful musician.
14. Do not make fun of our situation!
15. They made off with the profits.
16. Have you made up your mind yet?

B.
  1. (d)
  2. (a)
  3. (b)
  4. (c)
  5. (e)

Exercise Set 10-2

A.
  1. They have done well by their friends.
  2. I will do for him what I have done for you.
  3. Huge losses on the stock market did them in.
  4. Do up the buttons on your shirt!
  5. I cannot do without TV at night.
  6. We did away with that TV set because it was getting old.
  7. She does us proud because she is such a good person.
  8. Everyone must do their bit; otherwise it would not be fair.
  9. He always does his own thing, no matter who is with him.

B.
  1. You must go about your chores in a responsible way!
  2. I will not go along with anything you want to do.
  3. There's not enough food to go around.

4. They went at the job with a lot of energy.
5. As the years go by, I am becoming wiser.
6. How do you think my proposal will go down at the meeting?
7. I really go for the music of Beethoven.
8. His projects always go off smoothly.
9. Can you tell me what is going on?
10. At what time do you want to go out?
11. Go over the list and you'll see a pattern.
12. You should never go back on a promise.
13. A record number of retail stores went belly up last year.
14. Why not go for broke and start our own business?
15. Do you go for classical music?
16. To be truly independent, you must go it alone.
17. I always go out of my way for you.
18. She is someone who is clearly going places.
19. For how long have they been going steady?
20. It goes without saying that success is hard to come by without hard work.

Exercise Set 10-3

A.
1. She had on new shoes yesterday.
2. Mary, stay the course; otherwise you won't succeed!
3. We have a wedding party to go to tomorrow evening.
4. That car has had it. It is time to get a new one.
5. I know that my boss has it in for me, so I'm trying to avoid him.
6. OK, let's have it all out between the two of us. This is getting ridiculous.
7. You have had that scolding coming for a long time.
8. What you just said has nothing to do with what I'm saying.
9. For now, just stay put and don't go out with her!

B.
1. I looked on / upon her, mistakenly, as being on the other side.
2. If I don't look out, I may fall on the ice.
3. Where should I look you up?
4. Look alive! We are about to have some fun.
5. Don't be always looking down on my work, please!

6. We're looking forward to spending some time together.
7. Your new shoes make you look really sharp.
8. I have always looked up to my teachers.

Exercise Set 10-4

A.
1. getting along with people
2. getting around without a car
3. getting a point across
4. getting after someone to do something
5. getting across some point
6. getting away for relaxation
7. getting back from vacation
8. getting by with little money
9. getting down to work
10. getting in late
11. getting in with the wrong crowd
12. getting into trouble
13. getting off with a slap on the wrist
14. getting off early
15. getting on well with people
16. getting on in age
17. getting out a new book
18. getting over hard times

B.
1. (j)
2. (i)
3. (h)
4. (f)
5. (g)
6. (e)
7. (d)
8. (c)
9. (b)
10. (a)

Chapter 11

Exercise Set 11-1

A.
1. one hundred and two
2. five hundred and sixty-seven
3. one thousand two hundred and thirty-four
4. twenty-three thousand seven hundred and ninety-eight
5. one hundred thousand
6. one hundred and thirty-fourth
7. seven thousand eight hundred and ninetieth
8. one-seventh
9. three-fifths
10. half / one-half / a half

B.
1. I am around twenty-eight.
2. triple
3. twelve
4. 1 inch
5. 1 yard
6. 1 mile
7. 1 ounce
8. 1 pound
9. 1 pint
10. 1 gallon

Exercise Set 11-2

A.
1. It's six ten in the morning.
2. It's seven thirty in the evening.
3. It's (twelve) midnight.
4. It's (twelve) noon.
5. It's one fifty-five in the afternoon. / It's five to two in the afternoon.
6. It's nine fifteen in the morning. / It's a quarter past / after nine in the morning.

B.
1. morning
2. noon / midday
3. tonight
4. tomorrow
5. twenty minutes ago
6. watch
7. My watch is slow.
8. dial
9. It's three o'clock on the dot.

Exercise Set 11-3

A.
1. Sunday
2. Thursday
3. Wednesday
4. Tuesday
5. January and December
6. February
7. April
8. May
9. July
10. September
11. October
12. November
13. summer
14. winter
15. fall
16. spring

B.
1. on Saturdays
2. in September
3. ago
4. till / until
5. September (the) twenty-first
6. April (the) fourth

Exercise Set 11-4

A.
1. clap of thunder
2. blizzard
3. hurricane
4. It's freezing.
5. It's warm.

B.
1. south
2. west
3. northwest
4. southwest
5. sunset
6. twilight
7. It's sunny.
8. It's beautiful.
9. It's hot.

Exercise Set 11-5

A.
1. insane / mad
2. willingly / happily
3. a lot
4. zero
5. fast
6. identical
7. road
8. thus
9. really
10. know

B.
1. ugly
2. dirty
3. dark
4. difficult

5. full
6. exit
7. bad
8. outside
9. far
10. closed
11. poor
12. short

Exercise Set 11-6

A.

	Job / profession	Subject / discipline
violinist	✔	
anthropology		✔
carpenter	✔	
ethics		✔
electronics		✔
singer	✔	
tailor	✔	

B.
1. (b)
2. (a)
3. (b)
4. (a)
5. (a)
6. (a)
7. (a)

Chapter 12

Exercise Set 12-1

A.
1. I live in New York.
2. I am thirty years old.
3. My name is Gina Carletti.

4. I do not understand what you just said.
5. Can you speak more slowly?

B.
1. How are you?
2. Where do you live?
3. What's your name?
4. What time is it?
5. What's today's date? / What date is it?
6. How's the weather? / What's the weather like?
7. How old is he?

Exercise Set 12-2

A.
1. (a)
2. (b)
3. (b)
4. (a)
5. (a)

B.
1. With whom am I speaking?
2. Have a good day!
3. See you soon / later!
4. So long!
5. Take care!
6. Who is this / it?

Exercise Set 12-3

A.
1. Excuse me.
2. Thanks a lot / a million!
3. Glad to meet you.
4. A pleasure to make your acquaintance.
5. Allow me to introduce you to Julie Bergin.
6. Delighted / Glad to meet you.

B.
1. indifference
2. pity
3. disagreement
4. agreement
5. resignation
6. surprise
7. surprise

Chapter 13

Exercise Set 13-1

A.
1. I really dislike driving in rush hour traffic. It drives me insane!
2. I prefer walking to driving.
3. If you dislike baseball so much, why do you keep on watching it on TV?
4. I would like some sugar with my coffee, please.
5. I do not like tea; I prefer coffee.
6. You should enjoy your good life.
7. I relish pasta more than anything else.
8. She dotes on her children.

B.
1. I am very fond of playing the piano.
2. I love my friend.
3. I hate that song.
4. I really like good clothes.
5. She really dislikes going out.

Exercise Set 13-2

A.
1. (b)
2. (a)
3. (d)
4. (c)

5. (g)
6. (e)
7. (f)
8. (i)
9. (h)

B.
1. Let's go out right now, OK?
2. The game is supposed to begin soon.
3. Shall I call you tonight to set something up?
4. Where should we go? We could go to the park.
5. I know I should study more in order to become proficient in English.
6. I failed that test. I should have studied more.
7. If you're having trouble with grammar, you could try taking a course.

Exercise Set 13-3

A.
1. (g)
2. (f)
3. (e)
4. (a)
5. (b)
6. (c)
7. (d)

B.
1. We took in the sights of Chicago.
2. Did the plane take off on time?
3. You're taking on too much work.
4. I always take out my frustration by shouting at my dog.
5. Did she take over as director?
6. Take care of yourself.
7. The aspirins will start taking effect soon.
8. One should never take loved ones for granted.
9. Take all the time you need.
10. My ideas have finally taken root.
11. His ideas took shape a long time ago.
12. You should never take sides in arguments!

Chapter 14

Exercise Set 14-1

A.

	Formal	Informal
To Whom It May Concern:	✔	
Best wishes,		✔
Take care,		✔
Sincerely yours,	✔	
Yours sincerely,	✔	
With love,		✔
See you,		✔
Dear John,		✔
Dear Sir or Madam,	✔	
Respectfully yours,	✔	

B.

42 Michigan Avenue
Chicago, Illinois 60614

Mary Doolittle
34 Main Street
Memphis, Tennessee 38163

Exercise Set 14-2

A.
1. We went out, even though it was rather cold.
2. Is he coming as well?
3. Give me that pen right away!
4. Their apartment has long, narrow, dark corridors.
5. When he arrived, we decided to go out.
6. Ah, why did you do that?
7. She's here, isn't she?
8. "Please stay on the line," she said.

9. Staying calm is important; shouting is not.
10. She asked: "What's your name?"

B.
1. accommodate
2. acquire
3. believe
4. benefited
5. embarrass
6. existence
7. proceed
8. pursue
9. receive
10. similar
11. February
12. height
13. occurring
14. perceive
15. precede
16. achieve

Exercise Set 14-3

A.
1. (b)
2. (c)
3. (d)
4. (e)
5. (f)
6. (g)
7. (h)
8. (a)

B.
1. *2day*
2. *2U*
3. *b4*
4. *btw*
5. *cu*

6. *ez*
7. *gr8*
8. *gtg*
9. *nrn*
10. *thx*

Exercise Set 14-4

A.

Résumé

Jean McDowell

201 Pine Street
Milwaukee, WI 55428
USA
Tel.: (414) 787-7878
E-mail: jean.mcdowell@sympatico.com

Job Objective
  To find employment in the Milwaukee school system

Education
  B.A. in mathematics at the University of Wisconsin at Milwaukee
  High School Diploma, Kenosha, Wisconsin

Work Experience
  Teacher's assistant in several elementary schools in Milwaukee
  Volunteer at Youth Center in Kenosha
  Tutored high school students for 2 years

Other Details
  Member of Mensa
  Hobbies include playing the violin

References
  Available upon request

B.
1. (a)
2. (a)
3. (b)
4. (a)
5. (a)

Chapter 15

Exercise Set 15-1

A.
1. When we were in Florida, we went to the beach a lot.
2. Because he wanted to win first prize, he practiced a lot.
3. My cousins, many of whom live nearby, generally call me on weekends.
4. It is important that he study a lot for the exam.
5. She is the person who knows which movie we are supposed to see.
6. The book, whose title I have forgotten, is on the first shelf.
7. The idea that we have been discussing is an old one.

B.
1. Before leaving for the movies, they had a long conversation.
2. Since coming to San Francisco, they have made many friends.
3. The people sitting next to me at the opera were very noisy.
4. The woman sitting next to me is my mother.
5. The CD playing right now is by Frank Sinatra.
6. The ideas that are being discussed on that program are rather boring.

Exercise Set 15-2

A.
1. The boy remarked (that) he watched TV a lot.
2. She responded (that) she had not eaten anything.
3. I replied (that) I might eat later.
4. Jane commented (that) she had to get up early.
5. They added (that) they were going to go out just the same.
6. Jill confessed (that) she should work out more often.

B.
1. My friend said, "I go out a lot."
2. Mary responded, "I have not seen that movie."
3. She replied, "I might call later."
4. They complained, "We have to work all day."
5. They added, "We are going to speak out just the same."
6. My sister confessed, "I should study a lot more."

Exercise Set 15-3

A.
1. house, place
2. lab
3. ad
4. drink, booze
5. paper
6. children, kids
7. bucks
8. bye
9. hi

B.
1. T
2. T
3. T
4. T
5. F

Irregular Verbs

(to) arise

> Simple past (preterit): *(I) arose, (you) arose, (he) arose, (she) arose, (we) arose, (they) arose*
> Present participle: *arising*
> Past participle: *arisen*

(to) awake

> Simple past (preterit): *(I) awoke, (you) awoke, (he) awoke, (she) awoke, (we) awoke, (they) awoke*
> Present participle: *awaking*
> Past participle: *awoken*

(to) be

> Simple present: *(I) am, (you) are, (he) is, (she) is, (we) are, (they) are*
> Simple past (preterit): *(I) was, (you) were, (he) was, (she) was, (we) were, (they) were*
> Present participle: *being*
> Past participle: *been*

(to) be able to

> Simple present: *(I) can, (you) can, (he) can, (she) can, (we) can, (they) can*
> Simple past (preterit): *(I) could, (you) could, (he) could, (she) could, (we) could, (they) could*

(to) bear

> Simple past (preterit): *(I) bore, (you) bore, (he) bore, (she) bore, (we) bore, (they) bore*
> Past participle: *borne*

(to) beat

Simple past (preterit): *(I) beat, (you) beat, (he) beat, (she) beat, (we) beat, (they) beat*
Past participle: *beaten*

(to) become

Simple past (preterit): *(I) became, (you) became, (he) became, (she) became, (we) became, (they) became*
Present participle: *becoming*
Past participle: *become*

(to) begin

Simple past (preterit): *(I) began, (you) began, (he) began, (she) began, (we) began, (they) began*
Present participle: *beginning*
Past participle: *begun*

(to) bend

Simple past (preterit): *(I) bent, (you) bent, (he) bent, (she) bent, (we) bent, (they) bent*
Past participle: *bent*

(to) bet

Simple past (preterit): *(I) bet / betted, (you) bet / betted, (he) bet / betted, (she) bet / betted, (we) bet / betted, (they) bet / betted*
Present participle: *betting*
Past participle: *bet, betted*

(to) bid

Simple past (preterit): *(I) bid, (you) bid, (he) bid, (she) bid, (we) bid, (they) bid*
Present participle: *bidding*
Past participle: *bid*

(to) bind

> Simple past (preterit): *(I) bound, (you) bound, (he) bound, (she) bound, (we) bound, (they) bound*
> Past participle: *bound*

(to) bite

> Simple past (preterit): *(I) bit, (you) bit, (he) bit, (she) bit, (we) bit, (they) bit*
> Present participle: *biting*
> Past participle: *bitten*

(to) bleed

> Simple past (preterit): *(I) bled, (you) bled, (he) bled, (she) bled, (we) bled, (they) bled*
> Past participle: *bled*

(to) blow

> Simple past (preterit): *(I) blew, (you) blew, (he) blew, (she) blew, (we) blew, (they) blew*
> Past participle: *blown*

(to) break

> Simple past (preterit): *(I) broke, (you) broke, (he) broke, (she) broke, (we) broke, (they) broke*
> Past participle: *broken*

(to) breed

> Simple past (preterit): *(I) bred, (you) bred, (he) bred, (she) bred, (we) bred, (they) bred*
> Past participle: *bred*

(to) bring

> Simple past (preterit): *(I) brought, (you) brought, (he) brought, (she) brought, (we) brought, (they) brought*
> Past participle: *brought*

(to) build

Simple past (preterit): *(I) built, (you) built, (he) built, (she) built, (we) built, (they) built*
Past participle: *built*

(to) burn

Simple past (preterit): *(I) burnt / burned, (you) burnt / burned, (he) burnt / burned, (she) burnt / burned, (we) burnt / burned, (they) burnt / burned*
Past participle: *burnt / burned*

(to) burst

Simple past (preterit): *(I) burst, (you) burst, (he) burst, (she) burst, (we) burst, (they) burst*
Past participle: *burst*

(to) buy

Simple past (preterit): *(I) bought, (you) bought, (he) bought, (she) bought, (we) bought, (they) bought*
Past participle: *bought*

(to) catch

Simple past (preterit): *(I) caught, (you) caught, (he) caught, (she) caught, (we) caught, (they) caught*
Past participle: *caught*

(to) choose

Simple past (preterit): *(I) chose, (you) chose, (he) chose, (she) chose, (we) chose, (they) chose*
Present participle: *choosing*
Past participle: *chosen*

(to) cling

Simple past (preterit): *(I) clung, (you) clung, (he) clung, (she) clung, (we) clung, (they) clung*
Past participle: *clung*

(to) come

Simple past (preterit): *(I) came, (you) came, (he) came, (she) came, (we) came, (they) came*
Present participle: *coming*
Past participle: *come*

(to) cost

Simple past (preterit): *(it) cost, (they) cost*
Past participle: *cost*

(to) creep

Simple past (preterit): *(I) crept, (you) crept, (he) crept, (she) crept, (we) crept, (they) crept*
Past participle: *crept*

(to) cut

Simple past (preterit): *(I) cut, (you) cut, (he) cut, (she) cut, (we) cut, (they) cut*
Present participle: *cutting*
Past participle: *cut*

(to) deal

Simple past (preterit): *(I) dealt, (you) dealt, (he) dealt, (she) dealt, (we) dealt, (they) dealt*
Past participle: *dealt*

(to) dig

Simple past (preterit): *(I) dug, (you) dug, (he) dug, (she) dug, (we) dug, (they) dug*
Present participle: *digging*
Past participle: *dug*

(to) do

Simple present: *(I) do, (you) do, (he) does, (she) does, (we) do, (they) do*

Simple past (preterit): *(I) did, (you) did, (he) did, (she) did, (we) did, (they) did*

Past participle: *done*

(to) draw

Simple past (preterit): *(I) drew, (you) drew, (he) drew, (she) drew, (we) drew, (they) drew*

Past participle: *drew*

(to) dream

Simple past (preterit): *(I) dreamt / dreamed, (you) dreamt / dreamed, (he) dreamt / dreamed, (she) dreamt / dreamed, (we) dreamt / dreamed, (they) dreamt / dreamed*

Past participle: *dreamt / dreamed*

(to) drink

Simple past (preterit): *(I) drank, (you) drank, (he) drank, (she) drank, (we) drank, (they) drank*

Past participle: *drunk*

(to) drive

Simple past (preterit): *(I) drove, (you) drove, (he) drove, (she) drove, (we) drove, (they) drove*

Present participle: *driving*

Past participle: *driven*

(to) eat

Simple past (preterit): *(I) ate, (you) ate, (he) ate, (she) ate, (we) ate, (they) ate*

Past participle: *eaten*

(to) fall

Simple past (preterit): *(I) fell, (you) fell, (he) fell, (she) fell, (we) fell, (they) fell*
Past participle: *fallen*

(to) feed

Simple past (preterit): *(I) fed, (you) fed, (he) fed, (she) fed, (we) fed, (they) fed*
Past participle: *fed*

(to) feel

Simple past (preterit): *(I) felt, (you) felt, (he) felt, (she) felt, (we) felt, (they) felt*
Past participle: *felt*

(to) fight

Simple past (preterit): *(I) fought, (you) fought, (he) fought, (she) fought, (we) fought, (they) fought*
Past participle: *fought*

(to) find

Simple past (preterit): *(I) found, (you) found, (he) found, (she) found, (we) found, (they) found*
Past participle: *found*

(to) fit

Simple past (preterit): *(I) fitted / fit, (you) fitted / fit, (he) fitted / fit, (she) fitted / fit, (we) fitted / fit, (they) fitted / fit*
Present participle: *fitting*
Past participle: *fitted*

(to) flee

Simple past (preterit): *(I) fled, (you) fled, (he) fled, (she) fled, (we) fled, (they) fled*
Present participle: *fleeing*
Past participle: *fled*

(to) fling

Simple past (preterit): *(I) flung, (you) flung, (he) flung, (she) flung, (we) flung, (they) flung*
Past participle: *flung*

(to) fly

Simple past (preterit): *(I) flew, (you) flew, (he) flew, (she) flew, (we) flew, (they) flew*
Past participle: *flown*

(to) forbid

Simple past (preterit): *(I) forbad(e), (you) forbad(e), (he) forbad(e), (she) forbad(e), (we) forbad(e), (they) forbad(e)*
Present participle: *forbidding*
Past participle: *forbidden*

(to) forecast

Simple past (preterit): *(I) forecast, (you) forecast, (he) forecast, (she) forecast, (we) forecast, (they) forecast*
Past participle: *forecast*

(to) forget

Simple past (preterit): *(I) forgot, (you) forgot, (he) forgot, (she) forgot, (we) forgot, (they) forgot*
Present participle: *forgetting*
Past participle: *forgotten*

(to) forgive

Simple past (preterit): *(I) forgive, (you) forgive, (he) forgive, (she) forgive, (we) forgive, (they) forgive*
Present participle: *forgiving*
Past participle: *forgiven*

(to) freeze

Simple past (preterit): *(I) froze, (you) froze, (he) froze, (she) froze, (we) froze, (they) froze*
Present participle: *freezing*
Past participle: *frozen*

(to) get

Simple past (preterit): *(I) got, (you) got, (he) got, (she) got, (we) got, (they) got*
Present participle: *getting*
Past participle: *got, gotten*

(to) give

Simple past (preterit): *(I) gave, (you) gave, (he) gave, (she) gave, (we) gave, (they) gave*
Present participle: *giving*
Past participle: *given*

(to) go

Simple present: *(I) go, (you) go, (he) goes, (she) goes, (we) go, (they) go*
Simple past (preterit): *(I) went, (you) went, (he) went, (she) went, (we) went, (they) went*
Past participle: *gone*

(to) grind

Simple past (preterit): *(I) ground, (you) ground, (he) ground, (she) ground, (we) ground, (they) ground*
Past participle: *ground*

(to) grow

Simple past (preterit): *(I) grew, (you) grew, (he) grew, (she) grew, (we) grew, (they) grew*
Past participle: *grown*

(to) hang

> Simple past (preterit): *(I) hung, (you) hung, (he) hung, (she) hung, (we) hung, (they) hung*
> Past participle: *hung*

(to) have

> Simple present: *(I) have, (you) have, (he) has, (she) has, (we) have, (they) have*
> Simple past (preterit): *(I) had, (you) had, (he) had, (she) had, (we) had, (they) had*
> Present participle: *having*
> Past participle: *had*

(to) hear

> Simple past (preterit): *(I) heard, (you) heard, (he) heard, (she) heard, (we) heard, (they) heard*
> Past participle: *heard*

(to) hide

> Simple past (preterit): *(I) hid, (you) hid, (he) hid, (she) hid, (we) hid, (they) hid*
> Present participle: *hiding*
> Past participle: *hid*

(to) hit

> Simple past (preterit): *(I) hit, (you) hit, (he) hit, (she) hit, (we) hit, (they) hit*
> Present participle: *hitting*
> Past participle: *hit*

(to) hold

> Simple past (preterit): *(I) held, (you) held, (he) held, (she) held, (we) held, (they) held*
> Past participle: *held*

(to) hurt

Simple past (preterit): *(I) hurt, (you) hurt, (he) hurt, (she) hurt, (we) hurt, (they) hurt*
Past participle: *hurt*

(to) keep

Simple past (preterit): *(I) kept, (you) kept, (he) kept, (she) kept, (we) kept, (they) kept*
Past participle: *kept*

(to) kneel

Simple past (preterit): *(I) knelt, (you) knelt, (he) knelt, (she) knelt, (we) knelt, (they) knelt*
Past participle: *knelt*

(to) know

Simple past (preterit): *(I) knew, (you) knew, (he) knew, (she) knew, (we) knew, (they) knew*
Past participle: *known*

(to) lay

Simple past (preterit): *(I) laid, (you) laid, (he) laid, (she) laid, (we) laid, (they) laid*
Past participle: *laid*

(to) lead

Simple past (preterit): *(I) led, (you) led, (he) led, (she) led, (we) led, (they) led*
Past participle: *led*

(to) leave

Simple past (preterit): *(I) left, (you) left, (he) left, (she) left, (we) left, (they) left*
Present participle: *leaving*
Past participle: *left*

(to) lend

Simple past (preterit): *(I) lent, (you) lent, (he) lent, (she) lent, (we) lent, (they) lent*
Past participle: *arisen*

(to) let

Simple past (preterit): *(I) let, (you) let, (he) let, (she) let, (we) let, (they) let*
Present participle: *letting*
Past participle: *let*

(to) lie (recline)

Simple past (preterit): *(I) lay, (you) lay, (he) lay, (she) lay, (we) lay, (they) lay*
Present participle: *lying*
Past participle: *lain*

(to) light

Simple past (preterit): *(I) lit / lighted, (you) lit / lighted, (he) lit / lighted, (she) lit / lighted, (we) lit / lighted, (they) lit / lighted*
Past participle: *lit / lighted*

(to) lose

Simple past (preterit): *(I) lost, (you) lost, (he) lost, (she) lost, (we) lost, (they) lost*
Present participle: *losing*
Past participle: *lost*

(to) make

Simple past (preterit): *(I) made, (you) made, (he) made, (she) made, (we) made, (they) made*
Present participle: *making*
Past participle: *made*

may

> Simple past (preterit): (I) *might,* (you) *might,* (he) *might,* (she) *might,* (we) *might,* (they) *might*

(to) mean

> Simple past (preterit): (I) *meant,* (you) *meant,* (he) *meant,* (she) *meant,* (we) *meant,* (they) *meant*
> Past participle: *meant*

(to) meet

> Simple past (preterit): (I) *met,* (you) *met,* (he) *met,* (she) *met,* (we) *met,* (they) *met*
> Past participle: *met*

(to) mistake

> Simple past (preterit): (I) *mistook,* (you) *mistook,* (he) *mistook,* (she) *mistook,* (we) *mistook,* (they) *mistook*
> Present participle: *mistaking*
> Past participle: *mistaken*

(to) mow

> Past participle: *mown*

(to) pay

> Simple past (preterit): (I) *paid,* (you) *paid,* (he) *paid,* (she) *paid,* (we) *paid,* (they) *paid*
> Past participle: *paid*

(to) put

> Simple past (preterit): (I) *put,* (you) *put,* (he) *put,* (she) *put,* (we) *put,* (they) *put*
> Present participle: *putting*
> Past participle: *put*

(to) quit

Simple past (preterit): *(I) quit, (you) quit, (he) quit, (she) quit, (we) quit, (they) quit*
Present participle: *quitting*
Past participle: *quit*

(to) read

Simple past (preterit): *(I) read, (you) read, (he) read, (she) read, (we) read, (they) read*
Past participle: *read*

(to) rid

Simple past (preterit): *(I) rid, (you) rid, (he) rid, (she) rid, (we) rid, (they) rid*
Present participle: *ridding*
Past participle: *rid*

(to) ride

Simple past (preterit): *(I) rode, (you) rode, (he) rode, (she) rode, (we) rode, (they) rode*
Present participle: *riding*
Past participle: *ridden*

(to) ring

Simple past (preterit): *(I) rang, (you) rang, (he) rang, (she) rang, (we) rang, (they) rang*
Past participle: *rung*

(to) rise

Simple past (preterit): *(I) rose, (you) rose, (he) rose, (she) rose, (we) rose, (they) rose*
Present participle: *rising*
Past participle: *risen*

(to) run

Simple past (preterit): *(I) ran, (you) ran, (he) ran, (she) ran, (we) ran, (they) ran*
Present participle: *running*
Past participle: *run*

(to) say

Simple past (preterit): *(I) said, (you) said, (he) said, (she) said, (we) said, (they) said*
Past participle: *said*

(to) see

Simple past (preterit): *(I) saw, (you) saw, (he) saw, (she) saw, (we) saw, (they) saw*
Past participle: *seen*

(to) seek

Simple past (preterit): *(I) sought, (you) sought, (he) sought, (she) sought, (we) sought, (they) sought*
Past participle: *sought*

(to) sell

Simple past (preterit): *(I) sold, (you) sold, (he) sold, (she) sold, (we) sold, (they) sold*
Past participle: *sold*

(to) send

Simple past (preterit): *(I) sent, (you) sent, (he) sent, (she) sent, (we) sent, (they) sent*
Past participle: *sent*

(to) set

Simple past (preterit): *(I) set, (you) set, (he) set, (she) set, (we) set, (they) set*
Present participle: *setting*
Past participle: *set*

(to) shake

Simple past (preterit): *(I) shook, (you) shook, (he) shook, (she) shook, (we) shook, (they) shook*
Present participle: *shaking*
Past participle: *shaken*

(to) shed

Simple past (preterit): *(I) shed, (you) shed, (he) shed, (she) shed, (we) shed, (they) shed*
Present participle: *shedding*
Past participle: *shed*

(to) shine

Simple past (preterit): *(I) shone, (you) shone, (he) shone, (she) shone, (we) shone, (they) shone*
Present participle: *shining*
Past participle: *shone*

(to) shoot

Simple past (preterit): *(I) shot, (you) shot, (he) shot, (she) shot, (we) shot, (they) shot*
Past participle: *shot*

(to) show

Past participle: *shown*

(to) shrink

Simple past (preterit): *(I) shrank, (you) shrank, (he) shrank, (she) shrank, (we) shrank, (they) shrank*
Past participle: *shrunk*

(to) shut

Simple past (preterit): *(I) shut, (you) shut, (he) shut, (she) shut, (we) shut, (they) shut*
Present participle: *shutting*
Past participle: *shut*

(to) sing

Simple past (preterit): *(I) sang, (you) sang, (he) sang, (she) sang, (we) sang, (they) sang*
Past participle: *sung*

(to) sink

Simple past (preterit): *(I) sank, (you) sank, (he) sank, (she) sank, (we) sank, (they) sank*
Past participle: *sunk*

(to) sit

Simple past (preterit): *(I) sat, (you) sat, (he) sat, (she) sat, (we) sat, (they) sat*
Present participle: *sitting*
Past participle: *sat*

(to) sleep

Simple past (preterit): *(I) slept, (you) slept, (he) slept, (she) slept, (we) slept, (they) slept*
Past participle: *slept*

(to) slide

Simple past (preterit): *(I) slid, (you) slid, (he) slid, (she) slid, (we) slid, (they) slid*
Present participle: *sliding*
Past participle: *slid*

(to) sling

Simple past (preterit): *(I) slung, (you) slung, (he) slung, (she) slung, (we) slung, (they) slung*
Past participle: *slung*

(to) speak

Simple past (preterit): *(I) spoke, (you) spoke, (he) spoke, (she) spoke, (we) spoke, (they) spoke*
Past participle: *spoken*

(to) speed

Simple past (preterit): *(I) sped, (you) sped, (he) sped, (she) sped, (we) sped, (they) sped*
Past participle: *sped*

(to) spend

Simple past (preterit): *(I) spent, (you) spent, (he) spent, (she) spent, (we) spent, (they) spent*
Past participle: *spent*

(to) spin

Simple past (preterit): *(I) spun, (you) spun, (he) spun, (she) spun, (we) spun, (they) spun*
Present participle: *spinning*
Past participle: *spun*

(to) spit

Simple past (preterit): *(I) spat, (you) spat, (he) spat, (she) spat, (we) spat, (they) spat*
Present participle: *spitting*
Past participle: *spit*

(to) split

Simple past (preterit): *(I) split, (you) split, (he) split, (she) split, (we) split, (they) split*
Past participle: *split*

(to) spread

Simple past (preterit): *(I) spread, (you) spread, (he) spread, (she) spread, (we) spread, (they) spread*
Past participle: *spread*

(to) spring

Simple past (preterit): *(I) sprang, (you) sprang, (he) sprang, (she) sprang, (we) sprang, (they) sprang*
Past participle: *sprung*

(to) stand

Simple past (preterit): *(I) stood, (you) stood, (he) stood, (she) stood, (we) stood, (they) stood*
Past participle: *stood*

(to) steal

Simple past (preterit): *(I) stole, (you) stole, (he) stole, (she) stole, (we) stole, (they) stole*
Past participle: *stolen*

(to) stick

Simple past (preterit): *(I) stuck, (you) stuck, (he) stuck, (she) stuck, (we) stuck, (they) stuck*
Past participle: *stuck*

(to) sting

Simple past (preterit): *(I) stung, (you) stung, (he) stung, (she) stung, (we) stung, (they) stung*
Past participle: *stung*

(to) stink

Simple past (preterit): *(I) stank, (you) stank, (he) stank, (she) stank, (we) stank, (they) stank*
Past participle: *stunk*

(to) stride

Simple past (preterit): *(I) strode, (you) strode, (he) strode, (she) strode, (we) strode, (they) strode*
Present participle: *striding*
Past participle: *stridden*

(to) strike

Simple past (preterit): *(I) struck, (you) struck, (he) struck, (she) struck, (we) struck, (they) struck*
Present participle: *striking*
Past participle: *struck*

(to) strive

> Simple past (preterit): *(I) strove, (you) strove, (he) strove, (she) strove, (we) strove, (they) strove*
> Present participle: *striving*
> Past participle: *striven*

(to) swear

> Simple past (preterit): *(I) swore, (you) swore, (he) swore, (she) swore, (we) swore, (they) swore*
> Past participle: *sworn*

(to) sweep

> Simple past (preterit): *(I) swept, (you) swept, (he) swept, (she) swept, (we) swept, (they) swept*
> Past participle: *swept*

(to) swim

> Simple past (preterit): *(I) swam, (you) swam, (he) swam, (she) swam, (we) swam, (they) swam*
> Present participle: *swimming*
> Past participle: *swum*

(to) swing

> Simple past (preterit): *(I) swung, (you) swung, (he) swung, (she) swung, (we) swung, (they) swung*
> Past participle: *swung*

(to) take

> Simple past (preterit): *(I) took, (you) took, (he) took, (she) took, (we) took, (they) took*
> Present participle: *taking*
> Past participle: *taken*

(to) teach

>Simple past (preterit): (I) *taught, (you) taught, (he) taught, (she) taught, (we) taught, (they) taught*
>Past participle: *taught*

(to) tear

>Simple past (preterit): (I) *tore, (you) tore, (he) tore, (she) tore, (we) tore, (they) tore*
>Past participle: *torn*

(to) tell

>Simple past (preterit): (I) *told, (you) told, (he) told, (she) told, (we) told, (they) told*
>Past participle: *told*

(to) think

>Simple past (preterit): (I) *thought, (you) thought, (he) thought, (she) thought, (we) thought, (they) thought*
>Past participle: *thought*

(to) throw

>Simple past (preterit): (I) *threw, (you) threw, (he) threw, (she) threw, (we) threw, (they) threw*
>Past participle: *thrown*

(to) tread

>Simple past (preterit): (I) *trod, (you) trod, (he) trod, (she) trod, (we) trod, (they) trod*
>Past participle: *trodden*

(to) understand

>Simple past (preterit): (I) *understood, (you) understood, (he) understood, (she) understood, (we) understood, (they) understood*
>Past participle: *understood*

(to) upset

Simple past (preterit): *(I) upset, (you) upset, (he) upset, (she) upset, (we) upset, (they) upset*
Present participle: *upsetting*
Past participle: *upset*

(to) wake

Simple past (preterit): *(I) woke, (you) woke, (he) woke, (she) woke, (we) woke, (they) woke*
Present participle: *waking*
Past participle: *woken*

(to) wear

Simple past (preterit): *(I) wore, (you) wore, (he) wore, (she) wore, (we) wore, (they) wore*
Past participle: *worn*

(to) weave

Simple past (preterit): *(I) wove, (you) wove, (he) wove, (she) wove, (we) wove, (they) wove*
Present participle: *weaving*
Past participle: *woven*

(to) weep

Simple past (preterit): *(I) wept, (you) wept, (he) wept, (she) wept, (we) wept, (they) wept*
Past participle: *wept*

(to) win

Simple past (preterit): *(I) won, (you) won, (he) won, (she) won, (we) won, (they) won*
Present participle: *winning*
Past participle: *won*

(to) wind

Simple past (preterit): *(I) wound, (you) wound, (he) wound, (she) wound, (we) wound, (they) wound*
Past participle: *wound*

(to) withdraw

Simple past (preterit): *(I) withdrew, (you) withdrew, (he) withdrew, (she) withdrew, (we) withdrew, (they) withdrew*
Past participle: *withdrawn*

(to) write

Simple past (preterit): *(I) wrote, (you) wrote, (he) wrote, (she) wrote, (we) wrote, (they) wrote*
Present participle: *writing*
Past participle: *written*

Index